Full-Text (Substring) Indexes in External Memory

Synthesis Lectures on Data Management

Editor
M. Tamer Özsu, *University of Waterloo*

Synthesis Lectures on Data Management is edited by Tamer Özsu of the University of Waterloo. The series will publish 50- to 125 page publications on topics pertaining to data management. The scope will largely follow the purview of premier information and computer science conferences, such as ACM SIGMOD, VLDB, ICDE, PODS, ICDT, and ACM KDD. Potential topics include, but not are limited to: query languages, database system architectures, transaction management, data warehousing, XML and databases, data stream systems, wide scale data distribution, multimedia data management, data mining, and related subjects.

Full-Text (Substring) Indexes in External Memory
Marina Barsky, Ulrike Stege, Alex Thomo
2011

Spatial Data Management
Nikos Mamoulis
2011

Database Repairing and Consistent Query Answering
Leopoldo Bertossi
2011

Managing Event Information: Modeling, Retrieval, and Applications
Amarnath Gupta and Ramesh Jain
2011

Fundamentals of Physical Design and Query Compilation
David Toman and Grant Weddell
2011

Methods for Mining and Summarizing Text Conversations
Giuseppe Carenini, Gabriel Murray, and Raymond Ng
2011

Full-Text (Substring) Indexes in External Memory
Marina Barsky, Ulrike Stege, Alex Thomo

ISBN: 978-3-031-00757-6   paperback
ISBN: 978-3-031-01885-5   ebook

DOI 10.1007/978-3-031-01885-5

A Publication in the Springer series
SYNTHESIS LECTURES ON DATA MANAGEMENT

Lecture #22
Series Editor: M. Tamer Özsu, *University of Waterloo*
Series ISSN
Synthesis Lectures on Data Management
Print 2153-5418   Electronic 2153-5426

Full-Text (Substring) Indexes in External Memory

Marina Barsky, Ulrike Stege, Alex Thomo
University of Victoria

SYNTHESIS LECTURES ON DATA MANAGEMENT #22

ABSTRACT

Nowadays, textual databases are among the most rapidly growing collections of data. Some of these collections contain a new type of data that differs from classical numerical or textual data. These are long sequences of symbols, not divided into well-separated small tokens (words). The most prominent among such collections are databases of biological sequences, which are experiencing today an unprecedented growth rate. Starting in 2008, the "1000 Genomes Project" has been launched with the ultimate goal of collecting sequences of additional 1,500 Human genomes, 500 each of European, African, and East Asian origin. This will produce an extensive catalog of Human genetic variations. The size of just the raw sequences in this catalog would be about 5 terabytes.

Querying strings without well-separated tokens poses a different set of challenges, typically addressed by building *full-text indexes*, which provide effective structures to index all the substrings of the given strings. Since full-text indexes occupy more space than the raw data, it is often necessary to use disk space for their construction. However, until recently, the construction of full-text indexes in secondary storage was considered impractical due to excessive I/O costs. Despite this, algorithms developed in the last decade demonstrated that efficient external construction of full-text indexes is indeed possible.

This book is about large-scale construction and usage of full-text indexes. We focus mainly on *suffix trees*, and show efficient algorithms that can convert suffix trees to other kinds of full-text indexes and vice versa. There are four parts in this book. They are a mix of string searching theory with the reality of external memory constraints. The first part introduces general concepts of full-text indexes and shows the relationships between them. The second part presents the first series of external-memory construction algorithms that can handle the construction of full-text indexes for moderately large strings in the order of few gigabytes. The third part presents algorithms that scale for very large strings. The final part examines queries that can be facilitated by disk-resident full-text indexes.

KEYWORDS

full-text indexes, suffix trees, suffix arrays, external-memory algorithms, string pattern matching

For my father, Gennady, who lived to invent and to make things happen.

M.B.

For my family.

U.S.

For my wife, Mirela, and my sons, Jason and Ben.

A.T.

Contents

Preface

This book is about algorithms on strings. Strings are natural groupings of symbols into sequences, where the sequence adds a special significance that unsequenced groupings of symbols cannot convey. However, the book is not about strings in general, but about very long strings that lack clearly defined fragments (tokens). In practice, such long strings arise in music retrieval, Asian languages, and especially in databases of biological molecules, where the sequences of DNA bases and aminoacids are stored as long undivided strings of symbols. In addition, the book is not about algorithms that work on long strings *directly*, but about algorithms that pre-process the raw strings into useful structures (indexes) and enable efficient search and analysis. In essence, this requires the collections of strings to be static in order to enable the pre-processing. As such, this book is about algorithms that *build and use indexes for very long static strings*.

The goal of the book is primarily educational. We concentrate on the techniques that are important and at the same time can be explained with reasonable economy and efficiency, and which in turn can be converted into practical software applications.

The intended audience is senior undergraduate and graduate students in computer science, as well as software engineers. A basic knowledge of algorithms and memory hierarchies is required for reading this book. The ultimate goal is to provide the reader with new tools for developing practical software solutions for applications such as computational linguistics, music retrieval, and especially bioinformatics, where dealing with massive databases of strings is a daily occurrence.

In the first chapter we start by describing several data structures that can be used for indexing strings. At the end of this chapter we present the main challenge, namely the excessive memory requirement for full-text indexes and propose to solve this problem using external memory, typically magnetic disks. State-of-the-art construction algorithms for external memory are presented in Chapter 2. The extension of these algorithms to the case of input strings that do not fit into the main memory presents a major scalability challenge, and possible solutions for this case are discussed in Chapter 3. In Chapter 4 we discuss the efficiency of queries using disk-based indexes. Chapter 5 contains concluding remarks and suggestions for future work.

Marina Barsky, Ulrike Stege, Alex Thomo
November 2011

Acknowledgments

We owe our deepest gratitude to all the people who helped advance our research on disk-based full-text indexes: Tomas Bednar, Chris Upton, Michael Whitney, Valerie King, John Taylor, and Calisto Zuzarte. We wish to thank Tamer Ö for his encouragement to write this book and his insightful comments on the manuscript. We wish to thank our families for providing a loving environment, for their patience and endless support.

The work of Marina Barsky on this manuscript was supported in part by the Canadian Postdoctoral NSERC Fellowship PDF-388215.

Marina Barsky, Ulrike Stege, Alex Thomo
November 2011

CHAPTER 1

Structures for Indexing Substrings

1.1 INDEXING SUBSTRINGS

We begin by developing a general intuition of how we could index a very long string. First, we equip ourselves with some useful definitions.

Formally, we consider a *string* $X = x_1 x_2 \ldots x_N$ to be a sequence of N symbols (or characters) drawn from a finite alphabet Σ. We assume that X is represented as an array of characters. This allows to access any character at a given position i, $1 \leq i \leq N$, in constant time.

The consecutive sequence of symbols which starts at position i and ends at position j is called a *substring* $X[i, j]$ of X. We assume that $j \geq i$, and thus all substrings are non-empty strings and have a length of at least 1. To facilitate further discussion, we emphasize two special types of substrings: suffixes and prefixes.

A substring $[i, N]$ that starts at position i and runs to the end of X is called *suffix* S_i of X. Note that we can uniquely identify each suffix by its starting position i. Thus, $S_1 = X$ and $S_N = x_N$. *Prefix* P_i is substring $[1, i]$ of X. Thus, $P_1 = x_1$, and $P_N = X$. For example, for $X = banana$: $S_4 = ana$ (suffix starting at position 4), and $P_3 = ban$ (prefix ending at position 3).

If we can logically break X into small tokens (*words*), we then can sort these words and store them in a sorted list, attaching to each word the corresponding position where it occurs in X. In such a case, the search for a query word is facilitated, and we are able to locate the position of a query word by performing $\log N$ comparisons. This is the main principle behind an *inverted index*, which is widely used in information retrieval with applications to large collections of natural language texts.

Consider, however, a scenario where X cannot be logically partitioned into small words. Suppose that we would like to answer the following query on X: is a smaller string Q contained inside X, and if yes, at what position can it be found? For example, if $X = banana$ and $Q = nan$, the answer to this query is be position 3. The problem of locating a query string Q inside an input string X is called *exact pattern matching*.

Now, suppose that X is very large and static, and that the number of exact matching queries is large. This describes a typical scenario in the computational biology domain, where very long sequences of symbols represent molecular chains of DNA bases.

A naïve algorithm that searches for Q in a raw string X of size N incurs $O(N)$ string comparisons, and in each string comparison up to $|Q|$ character-to-character matchings, resulting in a time complexity $O(|Q|N)$. More sophisticated algorithms can find Q in X in time $O(N)$. Linear

b	a	n	a	n	a
1	2	3	4	5	6

Pos	2,4,6	2,4	2,4	2	2	1	1	1	1	1	1	3,5	3,5	3	3
Sub-string	a	a	a	a	a	b	b	b	b	b	b	n	n	n	n
		n	n	n	n		a	a	a	a	a		a	a	a
			a	a	a			n	n	n	n			n	n
				n	n				a	a	a				a
					a					n	n				
											a				

Figure 1.1:   Indexing all different substrings of $X = banana$.

time is also the lower bound of these algorithms because we need to read each character of X at least once. However, since we assume that X is static, we can pre-process the string and prepare an index that facilitates a subsequent *sub-linear* search.

Similarly, to the inverted index idea, we can build a sorted list of all different substrings of X. There are at most $N(N-1)/2$ distinct entries in this index: for each start position i, there are $N-i$ end positions. Each entry contains up to N characters. As a result, the total size of such a substring index is $O(N^3)$. An example of the substring index for $X = banana$ is shown in Figure 1.1. We are now able to locate any substring performing $O(log(N^2))$ string comparisons. However, even for the above string of 6 characters, the index contains 15 entries, with multiple position numbers per entry. Note, that some of these entries are redundant. For example, to locate substring *ana*, we need to locate only the suffixes that contain *ana* as a prefix, namely *ana* and *anana*. This leads to a general idea: in order to locate all different substrings of X, it is sufficient to build a sorted list of all suffixes of X.

An array of sorted suffixes for $X = banana$ is shown in Figure 1.2. Here, the number of entries is N – one entry per suffix. The search is performed using $O(\log N)$ string comparisons. However, the size of this sorted array is still quadratic in N. This is because each character at position i is repeated $N-i$ times. If we assume that we can read each character directly from X in constant time, then we only need to know at what position to read the character. Hence, we can replace each suffix in the sorted array by its starting position. The array of sorted suffixes in Figure 1.2 is represented as an array of numbers [6, 4, 2, 1, 5, 3]. When searching for $Q = ana$, we do a binary search using the array of suffix start positions, but we compare Q to the corresponding characters from X. After locating the first occurrence of *ana*, we collect the remaining occurrences by comparing *ana* to the suffixes to the left and to the right in this array.

An array of suffix start positions, arranged according to the lexicographic order of the suffixes that these positions represent, is called a *suffix array*. The suffix array is the first representative of a family of indexes that allow us to index all different substrings. These are called *full-text indexes*.

b	a	n	a	n	a
1	2	3	4	5	6

Pos	6	4	2	1	5	3
Suffix	a	a	a	b	n	n
		n	n	a	a	a
		a	a	n		n
			n	a		a
			a	n		
				a		

Figure 1.2:   The sorted suffixes of $X = banana$.

Note that all different full-text indexes presented in this chapter are based on the idea of sorted suffixes.

1.2   SUFFIX ARRAY

The suffix array of string X, introduced in the previous section, represents an index of all distinct substrings of X. Using binary search, we can search for any query string Q in time $O(|Q| \log N)$, matching up to $|Q|$ characters to at most $\log N$ suffixes. Moreover, in order to retrieve all occurrences of Q, we additionally check adjacent suffixes to the left and to the right of the first occurrence in the suffix array. If the length of Q is large and if Q occurs multiple times, we would like to enhance our index to avoid multiple scannings of the same characters. However, at each position we start a character-by-character comparison from scratch.

When considering the example in Figure 1.2, we notice that some adjacent suffixes share common prefixes. If this information would be available during the search, we could skip these characters, knowing that they are the same and we have already compared our query string to them. For example, suffixes $S_4 = ana$ and $S_2 = anana$ have in common prefix a, prefix an and prefix ana. The longest among these common prefixes is called *longest common prefix* (LCP) of two strings. Now, for each suffix S_i, represented by its start position, we add the length of the LCP of S_i with its predecessor in the suffix array. As a result, we obtain an *enhanced suffix array* that represents all the sorted suffixes of string X, where each suffix is represented by two numbers: its start position in X and the length of the LCP of this suffix with its predecessor. Figure 1.3 shows an example of such an array for string *banana*. The length of the LCP is denoted by lcp in further discussion.

Using the concept of LCP, binary search can be performed in time $O(|Q| + \log N)$. For each suffix S_i that is to be compared with Q, $lcp(S_i, Q)$ is computed. As long as lcp is zero, only one character is compared during this negative comparison. Once the interval for Q is located, say, between suffixes S_i and S_j, and the value of lcp between both Q and S_i and Q and S_j is greater than

b	a	n	a	n	a
1	2	3	4	5	6

Suffix	a	a	a	b	n	n
		n	n	a	a	a
		a	a	n		n
			n	a		a
			a	n		
				a		
Pos	6	4	2	1	5	3
lcp	0	1	3	0	0	2

Figure 1.3:   **[Top]** Sorted suffixes and longest common prefixes (LCPs) for $X = banana$. **[Bottom]** A suffix array of X enhanced with the lengths of the LCPs.

zero, all the suffixes between S_i and S_j share a LCP of length $a = min(lcp(Q, S_i), lcp(Q, S_j))$ due to the fact that the suffixes are lexicographically sorted. Hence, for subsequent comparisons we can start comparing characters in Q starting at position $a + 1$. As such, at most $2|Q|$ characters are matched in total. An example for a longer string is shown in Figure 1.4.

The LCP array itself helps to efficiently locate multiple occurrences. Once the first occurrence is found, the rest is collected by considering all adjacent suffixes where lcp values are at least $|Q|$, and no additional character comparisons are involved.

This concludes our description of the enhanced suffix array. In the next sections we introduce more advanced indexing structures where sorted suffixes are organized into trees. This adds additional functionality to our substring index.

1.3   SUFFIX TRIE

To introduce the idea of organizing suffixes into a tree, we sort all suffixes of a string $X = ababc$, initialize the root of the tree, and add each suffix as a path of nodes, one character per node, labeling each edge by the corresponding character. For instance, when adding suffix $S_3 = abc$, we notice that its prefix ab already exists as a descendant of the root node. Therefore, we do not add duplicate path ab, but instead we follow the existing sequence of nodes until characters do not match anymore. At this point we create a new child node for character c. The end node of a path for each suffix (a leaf node) is labeled with the starting position of the corresponding suffix in X. The result of this suffix arrangement for $X = ababc$ is shown in Figure 1.5. This digital tree of suffixes is called a *suffix trie*. For an input string over alphabet Σ, the maximum number of children for each trie node is $|\Sigma|$, and all children of a particular node must represent distinct symbols. Beginning at the root node, each of the suffixes of X can be found in the trie: $ababc$, $babc$, abc, bc and c. Because of this organization, the occurrence in X of any query string Q can be found by starting at the root and following matches

a	b	a	b	c	a	b	a	b
1	2	3	4	5	6	7	8	9

Suffix	a	a	a	a	b	b	b	b	c
	b	b	b	b	a	a	c		a
	a	a	c		b	b	a		b
	b	b	a		c		b		a
	c		b		a		a		b
	a		a		b		b		
	b		b		a				
	a				b				
	b								
Pos	1	6	3	8	2	7	4	9	5
lcp	0	4	2	2	0	3	1	1	0

Figure 1.4: Example of a binary search in the suffix array for $X = ababcabab$ and query string $Q = abca$. During the binary search we calculated $lcp(Q, S_6) = 2$ and $lcp(Q, S_8) = 2$. All the suffixes between S_6 and S_8 in this suffix array share a common prefix of length 2. This allows us to compare characters in Q and characters in the remaining suffixes starting from the third position in each of them.

down the trie edges until the query is exhausted. If the entire string Q has been matched, then the corresponding positions can be read by traversing the induced sub-tree in a depth-first manner.

Note that a similar arrangement does not work for string $X = abab$. In this case, suffix $S_3 = ab$ is a prefix of another suffix, $S_1 = abab$. As such, we do not have a separate leaf for $S_3 = ab$ and its starting position 3 is lost. In order to solve this problem, for a given input string X over alphabet Σ one additional character is appended to the end of X. This character is unique and not in Σ. This special character is called a *sentinel*. This ensures that an additional edge will be generated for a sentinel character and thus each start position will have its own leaf node. In our example for $X = ababc$, c serves as a sentinel due to its unique occurrence at the end of the input string. Since, for our indexing purposes, we treat the suffix trie as a tree of sorted suffixes, we consider the artificial sentinel character added to the end of X as being lexicographically the *smallest* among all characters in Σ. As such the sentinel essentially represents an empty string: ab is lexicographically smaller than $abab$.

The trie provides an efficient solution to the *substring containment problem*, i.e., answering whether or not a query string Q is a substring of X. To answer this, it takes exactly $|Q|$ character comparisons. This is a significant improvement over the $O(|Q| + \log N)$ result for suffix arrays. However, while the size of a suffix array is linear in N, the size of a suffix trie is $O(N^2)$. This worst

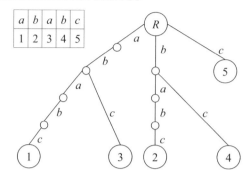

Figure 1.5:   The suffix *trie* for $X = ababc$. Since c occurs only at the end of X, it can serve as a unique sentinel symbol. Note that each suffix of X can be found in the trie by concatenating character labels on the path from the root to the corresponding leaf node.

case situation arises, for example, when all the paths in the trie are disjoint, as it is the case for input string *abcde*. This not only presents a difficulty for handling a quadratic-size index for a very long input string X, but it also makes the complete solution of the exact matching problem inefficient: after matching all characters of a query string Q to a path in the trie, collecting all occurrences can take time $O(N^2)$, since we need to traverse all the branches of the sub-tree induced by the original path, character-by-character.

In the next section we show how we can modify this data structure to make it suitable for solving our main problem. namely indexing substrings of a very long input string X.

1.4   SUFFIX TREE

The number of edges in the suffix trie can be reduced by collapsing paths containing unary nodes into a single edge. This process yields a structure called the *suffix tree*. Figure 1.6 [Right] shows how the suffix trie for $X = ababc$ looks like when converted to a suffix tree. The tree still has the same general shape, but far fewer nodes. As before, the leaves are labeled with the start position in X of the corresponding suffix, and each suffix can be found in the tree by concatenating substrings associated with edge labels. The total number of nodes in the suffix tree is constrained due to two facts: (1) there are exactly N leaves and (2) the degree of any external node is at least 2. Therefore, there are at most $N - 1$ internal nodes in the tree. Hence, the maximum number of nodes is linear in N. However, the problem of how to avoid an overall quadratic space is not yet resolved: the labels in the suffix tree contain exactly the same number of characters as the suffix trie.

Assuming that we can read any character at a given position directly from X in constant time, the substrings that label the edges of a suffix tree do not have to be stored explicitly. Instead, they can be represented as an ordered pair of integers indexing their start and end position in X. This implicit representation of substrings by their positions makes the total space occupied by the suffix

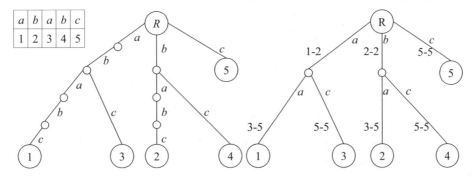

Figure 1.6: **[Left]** The suffix *trie* for $X = ababc$. **[Right]** The suffix tree for $X = ababc$. For clarity, the explicit edge labels are shown. They are represented as ordered pairs of positions in the actual suffix tree. Each suffix S_i can be found by concatenating substrings of X on the path from the root to leaf node L_i.

tree linear in N: now each edge label can be stored in a constant space, and there are at most $2N$ nodes (and edges).

In a nutshell, a *suffix tree* is a tree of symbols for the suffixes of X, where edges are labeled with the start and end positions of the substrings they represent in X. Note also that each internal node in the suffix tree represents the end of the longest common prefix for some pair of suffixes.

Exact pattern matching using suffix trees can be performed very efficiently. In fact, each query string Q can be located in X by following the path of symbols from the root of the suffix tree for X. The substring containment problem, namely whether Q is a substring of X, can be solved in time proportional to the length of query string Q and *independent* of the size of the pre-processed input. An example of such a search is shown in Figure 1.7. In order to report all occurrences occ of Q, the subtree induced by the end of the corresponding path is traversed, which results in a search with an optimal performance of $O(|Q| + occ)$. This result makes the suffix tree data structure the top candidate for our substring index.

Notably, the suffix tree index can be used to answer additional multiple combinatorial queries about input string X. For example, with help of the suffix tree we can count the total number of distinct substrings of the input string. This application is based on a fundamental property of the suffix tree: every distinct substring of input string X is spelled out exactly once along a path from the root of the suffix tree. Thus, an inventory of all the distinct substrings of X can be produced by listing all the strings along each such path. The total number of distinct substrings may be quadratic in input length, since in the worst case there may be as many as $O(N^2)$ distinct substrings in an input of size N (i.e., there are that many ways to choose the pair of start and end positions). However, the total *number* of all distinct substrings can be computed in time linear in N by simply adding up the lengths of the edges of the suffix tree. For example, there are 12 different substrings in string $ababc$, as can be calculated from the suffix tree in Figure 1.6 [Right].

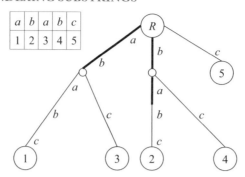

Figure 1.7: Examples of search in a suffix tree. The query strings *ab* and *ba* are found on the paths from the root of the tree (bold lines). Once the query string is located, the positions – (1, 3) for *ab* and (2) for *ba* – are obtained from the leaves of the corresponding subtrees.

Additional types of queries are discussed in Chapter 4 of this book. In fact, theoretically optimal bounds were obtained for many non-trivial tasks, such as computing matching statistics, locating all repetitive substrings, and extracting palindromes. As we read on page 122 in the book by Gusfield [1997]: "Perhaps the best way to appreciate the power of suffix trees is ... to spend some time trying to solve [these] problems without using suffix trees. Without this effort and without some historical perspective, the availability of suffix trees may make certain problems appear trivial, even though linear-time algorithms for those problems were unknown before the advent of suffix trees."

From this inspiring note, we now move on to a more practical question: how can we represent the suffix tree in (computer) memory?

1.5   REPRESENTATION OF A SUFFIX TREE

We discuss next the suffix tree representation in memory in order to estimate its space requirements in practice.

It is common to represent the node of a suffix tree together with the information about the incoming edge label. Each node, therefore, contains two integers representing the start and end position of the corresponding substring of X. In fact, it is sufficient to store only the start position of this substring as the end position can be deduced from the start position of the child (for an internal node) or it is simply N (for a leaf node). In a straightforward implementation, each node has pointers to all its child nodes. These child pointers can be represented as an array, as a linked list or as a hash table.

If the size $|\Sigma|$ of alphabet Σ is small, the child node pointers can be represented as an array of size $|\Sigma|$. Each ith entry in this array represents the child node whose incoming label starts with the ith character in the ranked alphabet. This is very useful for tree traversals, since the corresponding child can be located in constant time. Let us first consider the tree space for inputs where N is less than the largest 4-byte integer, i.e., $\log N < 32$. In this case, each node structure consists of $|\Sigma|$ integers for child node pointers plus one integer to represent the start position of the edge-label substring. Since there are at most $2N$ nodes in the tree, the total space required is $2N(|\Sigma| + 1)$ integers. For the example where $|\Sigma| = 4$ (e.g., DNA alphabet), this yields $40N$ bytes of storage per N bytes of input. An *array representation* of the suffix tree for $X = ababc$ is shown in Figure 1.8.

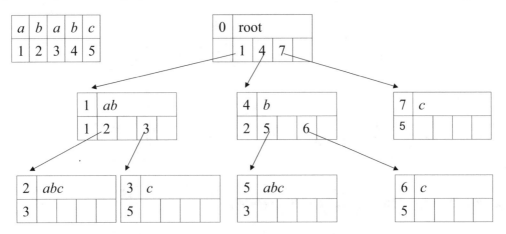

Figure 1.8: An array representation of the suffix tree for $X = ababc$. Each node contains an array of 4 child pointers. Note that not all the cells of this array are in use. The strings in the nodes are the labels of the incoming edges. They are shown for clarity only and are not stored explicitly.

For larger alphabets, an array representation of children is impractical and can be replaced by a linked list representation. However, this requires an additional $O(\log|\Sigma|)$ search time spent at each internal node during the tree traversal, in order to locate the corresponding child. In addition, since the position of a child in a list does not reflect the first symbol of its incoming edge label, we may need to store an additional byte representing this first character. Another possibility is to represent child pointers as a hash table. This preserves a constant-time access to each child node and is more space-efficient than the array representation.

The linked-list based representation known as a *left-child right-sibling* helps to further reduce the space. In this implementation, the suffix tree is represented as a set of node structures, each consisting of the start position of the substring labeling the incoming edge, together with two pointers – one pointing to the node's first child and the other one to its next sibling. Recall that the end position of the edge-label substring is not stored explicitly, since for an internal node it can be deduced from the start position of its first child, and for a leaf node this end position is simply N. This representation of the node's children is of type linked list, with all its space advantages and search drawbacks. This suffix tree representation is illustrated in Figure 1.9. Each suffix tree node consists of three integers. Since there are up to $2N$ nodes in the tree, the size of such a tree is at most

$24N$. Again, for the better traversal efficiency, we store the first symbol along each edge label. Then the total size of a suffix tree is at most $25N$ bytes for N bytes of input.

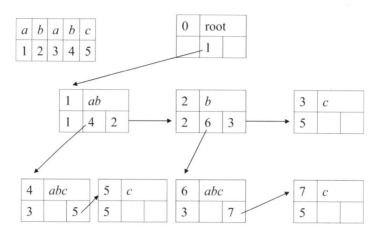

Figure 1.9: *Left-child right-sibling* representation of the suffix tree for $X = ababc$. Each node contains 1 pointer to its first child and 1 pointer to the next sibling.

In an even more space efficient storage scheme, the pointers to sibling nodes are not stored. Instead, the sibling nodes are placed consecutively in memory. The last sibling is marked by a special bit. Now, each node stores only the start position of a corresponding edge-label plus the pointer to its leftmost child. As before, each node may include an additional byte representing the start symbol of its edge label. The size of such a tree node is 9 bytes. For $2N$ nodes this yields a maximum of $18N$ bytes of storage. This representation is depicted in Figure 1.10.

a	*b*	*a*	*b*	*c*
1	2	3	4	5

Array index	0	1	2	3	4	5	6	7
Starting character		*a*	*b*	*c*	*a*	*c*	*a*	*c*
First child	1	4	6	L	L	L	L	L
Start pos		1	2	5*	3	5*	3	5*

Figure 1.10: Optimized *left-child right-sibling* representation of the suffix tree. All siblings are represented as consecutive elements in the array of nodes. The special symbol ⋆ marks the bit which indicates the last sibling. Each node contains only a pointer to the first child and the start position of the incoming edge-label.

Another possibility to optimize the storage of the suffix tree is to consider each suffix as a sequence of bits. Note that a string over any alphabet Σ can be reduced to the binary alphabet by representing each character as a sequence of $b = log|\Sigma|$ bits and then concatenating these binary sequences.

For a binary alphabet, any internal node in the suffix tree has exactly two children. This is because such a node cannot have more than two children, but also cannot have less than two for it to be a suffix tree internal node. This allows using two child pointers only (per node) and representing the entire suffix tree as an array of constant-sized nodes. If the entire input string is considered as a sequence of bits, only the *valid* suffixes are added to the tree. These are the suffixes starting at positions i such that $i \mod b = 0$, where b is the number of bits used to represent each character of Σ. As such, we have the same number of tree nodes as before: the tree has one leaf node and one internal node per inserted suffix. Figure 1.11 shows equivalent suffix trees over the original and the binary alphabets for input string $X = ababc$. Each node has exactly two child pointers plus one integer representing the start position of the incoming edge-label. Since there are exactly $2N$ nodes in such a tree, the total size is $24N$ bytes. Note that this result is independent of the size of the alphabet.

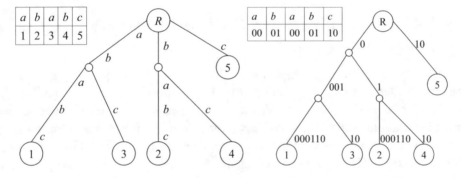

Figure 1.11:   **[Left]** Conventional suffix tree for $X = ababc$. **[Right]** Suffix tree for the same input string. Here, each suffix is converted to a sequence of bits. Each character is encoded using 2 bits.

This binary representation of the suffix tree efficiently supports multiple string queries. For example, in order to find occurrences of a pattern in string X, we can treat the pattern as a sequence of bits, and match these bits along the path starting at the root, without having the problem of locating the corresponding child of each internal node, as in linked-list-based representations.

Note that in all representations described above the leaf nodes do not need to store child pointers. Thus, we can store the leaf nodes in a separate array. Each element in the array of leaf nodes stores only the start position of the corresponding substring since the end position is implied to be N. In this case, the array representation occupies $24N$ bytes (for $|\Sigma| = 4$), the "left-child right-sibling" representation occupies $20N$ bytes, its optimized version occupies $12N$ bytes, and the suffix tree over the binary alphabet occupies $16N$ bytes.

The suffix tree, theoretically, is a compact index, since it stores in linear-space the total quadratic number of distinct substrings of X. However, this short survey of storage requirements clearly demonstrates that, in practice, the suffix tree index is very space-demanding. For example, for an input of 2 GB, the tree requires at least 24 GB of memory. Further, for inputs exceeding in size the largest 4-byte integer, the start positions and the child pointers need more than 4 bytes for their representation, namely log N bits for each number. In practice, for the inputs of a size in the tens of gigabytes the tree can easily reach $50N$ bytes. Recall that for the most space efficient representation of the suffix tree discussed so far, for an input of size 6 GB, we need at least 72 GB of storage space. Real inputs, however, may often be much larger than 6 GB. For example, the genome of Lilium longiflorum (trumpet lily) alone is 90 GB in size, and converting this input string into a suffix tree requires more than 1 TB of memory.

Due to these excessive memory requirements, large suffix trees cannot be constructed and stored entirely in RAM, and the power of suffix trees for very large inputs until recently has remained largely unharnessed.

There are two main directions in making suffix trees scalable for large inputs: the index compression and the use of disk space.

1.6   POSSIBLE SOLUTIONS TO THE MEMORY PROBLEM

1.6.1   INDEX COMPRESSION

The recently developed parenthesis representation (or *compressed suffix tree*) allows the entire suffix tree to be stored using only $5N$ *bits*. An example of the parenthesis representation of the suffix tree nodes for string $X = ababc$ is shown in Figure 1.12. The parentheses describe the tree topology. In order to store the information about the start position and the depth of each tree node, a special array and its unary encoding are used to bring the total memory requirements for the tree to $5N$ bits. The compressed suffix tree supports all regular suffix tree queries with a poly-log slowdown. Compressed suffix trees and arrays represent conceptually new *self-indexing* structures that do not require to access the input string for a search or traversal. The resulting compressed self-index is smaller than the original input and must be kept entirely in the main memory during the search. For example, the compressed suffix tree for 3 GB of Human genome occupies only 2 GB. These impressive results show that the entire fully-functional suffix tree can be stored using a lot less space than previously believed.

Thus, if the size of the main memory permits, a compressed full-text index can be developed. However, the scalability of compressed suffix trees does not go beyond inputs that are smaller than the main memory, since the index itself has a size in the same order of magnitude as the input it is built upon, and it must be completely loaded into RAM to be useful. If the compressed index outgrows the main memory and is accessed from disk, then severe disk thrashing occurs due to very poor locality of references.

More problematic from a practical point of view is the fact that algorithms for search in compressed indexes perform with a poly-log slowdown factor compared to the optimal algorithms

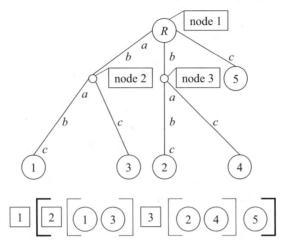

Figure 1.12: The compressed suffix tree for $X = ababc$ is shown below its conventional suffix tree. It uses parenthesis to represent the tree topology, and the storage space is reduced to $5N$ bits. However, queries on a compressed suffix tree are more complex and significantly slower than queries on the conventional suffix tree.

on uncompressed indexes. For example, the traversal of a compressed suffix tree for 3 GB of Human genome is 90 times slower than the traversal of a conventional suffix tree. The poly-log slowdown becomes even more prominent for larger input sizes.

Aiming to develop a *practical* solution, we do not consider compressed suffix trees in this book, but rather concentrate on the idea of using external memory for both tree construction and search.

1.6.2 USING DISK SPACE

Consider the idea of using disk space to store intermediate and resulting data structures during the suffix tree construction and during queries, without ever loading the entire index into main memory. Such a solution is quite attractive since disk space is cheap and virtually unlimited: we can hold on disks several terabytes of data.

For the use of disk to be efficient we need to take into account some properties of memory hierarchies.

There are several categories of memory in a computer ranging from small and fast to cheap and slow. The access to data on a disk is 10^5-10^6 times slower than the access to data in main memory. In order to model these speed differences in the design of algorithms that use external memory, the external memory computational model, or **d**isk **a**ccess **m**odel (DAM), was proposed. DAM represents the computer memory in the form of two layers with different access characteristics: the fast main memory of a limited size M, and a slow and arbitrarily large secondary storage memory (disk). In addition, for disks, it takes about as long to fetch a consecutive block of data as it does to fetch a single byte. This is why in the DAM model the asymptotic performance is evaluated as the total number of block transfers between a disk and main memory.

Although DAM is a workable approximation, it does not always accurately predict the performance of algorithms that use disk space. This is because DAM does not take into account an important disk access property described below. The cost of a *random* disk access is the sum of the seek time, rotational delay and transfer time. The first two dominate this cost in the average case, and as such are the bottleneck of a random disk I/O. However, if the disk head is positioned exactly over the piece of data we want, then there are neither seek time nor rotational delay components, but only transfer time. Hence, if we access data *sequentially* on disk, then we pay the seek time and rotational delay only for locating the first block of our data, but not for the subsequent blocks. The difference in cost between sequential and random access becomes even more prominent if we also consider read-ahead-buffering optimizations that are common in current disks and operating systems.

In fact, the real time of data transfer from disk and from RAM differs significantly depending on access patterns. Figure 1.13 represents the results of experiments, presented in the recent literature, on data transfer speeds for different memories. These results notably show that sequential disk access is even faster than random access to main memory. Therefore, if we design disk-based algorithms that are truly sequential, then we can potentially outperform algorithms that incur many random accesses to main memory.

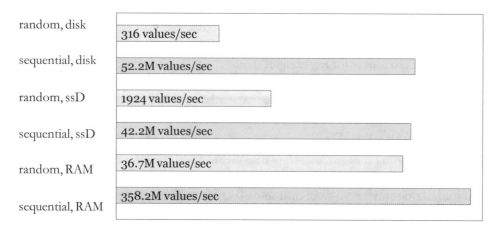

Figure 1.13: Data transfer speed for different memories (from Jacobs [2009]).

How do we efficiently construct a full text index using disk space? Note that we use the disk not only to store our index, but also as an extension to the amount of RAM used during its construction. Can we use the same algorithm as for the construction of an index entirely in main memory? We explore answers to these questions in the next chapter.

1.7   SUMMARY

We presented suffix-based indexing structures for indexing substrings of long input strings: suffix arrays, suffix tries and suffix trees. From these three, the most useful is the suffix tree that can be efficiently used not only for exact pattern search but also for more sophisticated queries. We discussed the high memory requirements of suffix trees and possible solutions to the memory problem: index compression and the use of disk space. For practical reasons, we have chosen to use the disk space as the extension of working memory for construction and querying of suffix trees. We discussed the requirements for disk-friendly suffix tree construction, namely sequential access to disk-resident data.

1.8   BIBLIOGRAPHIC NOTES

Historically, the *trie* concept was introduced first. The term trie as a type of a digital search tree for a set of strings was coined by Fredkin [1960] from information reTRIEval for a table-based implementation, and the structure was also independently proposed by de la Briandais de la Briandais [1959]. The term *suffix tree* first appears in the work by McCreight [1976]. An early, implicit form is to be found in Morrison's *PATRICIA tree* (Practical Algorithm To Retrieve Information Coded In Alphanumeric, Morrison [1968]), but it was Weiner [1973] who proposed to use it as explicit index. Suffix arrays were first introduced by Manber and Myers [1993].

Numerous algorithms that use suffix trees can be found in the book by Gusfield [1997], which also contains references to the original works.

The "left-child right-sibling" suffix tree representation was proposed by McCreight [1976]. An even more space efficient storage optimization was proposed by Giegerich et al. [2003]. Until 2007, the data structure by Giegerich et al. [2003] was known as the most space efficient representation of the suffix tree. Then Sadakane [2007] fully developed the compressed suffix tree and its balanced parenthesis representation. The use of the compressed suffix tree index for querying massive inputs was studied in the work of Fischer et al. [2008b]. More about compressed suffix trees can be found in recent papers by Fischer et al. [2008a] and Russo et al. [2008].

The external memory computational model, or **d**isk **a**ccess **m**odel (DAM), was proposed by Vitter and Shriver [1994].

CHAPTER 2

External Construction of Suffix Trees

In this chapter, we describe techniques for the efficient construction of disk-based full-text indexes. We start by showing that different kinds of indexes can be transformed into each other efficiently (Section 2.1). Therefore, a construction algorithm that is efficient for one type of index works for all others, too. Then, in Section 2.2, we introduce a simplest brute-force algorithm for the construction of suffix trees, and its optimization for external memory. In Section 2.3, we present an efficient in-memory algorithm for suffix tree construction, the Ukkonen algorithm. We show that the nearly random accesses inherent in this algorithm make it less suitable for external construction. Finally, in Section 2.4, we present three algorithms specifically designed to build suffix trees directly on disk. We conclude by describing the scalability problem of the presented algorithms, the problem which we address in Chapter 3.

Before we begin, let us refresh some basic terms that we use in the description of construction algorithms. For clarity, we assume that the input is represented as a single string X of size N. However, all the techniques presented here can be trivially extended to the case when the input consists of a set of strings of total length N.

We remind that suffix S_i is a substring of X which starts at position i and ends at position N. The longest common prefix $LCP_{i,j}$ is the prefix that is shared among two suffixes S_i and S_j. We denote the length of the LCP by lcp. A suffix array SA is an array of lexicographically sorted suffixes of X, where each suffix is represented by its start position. An LCP array is an array of lcp values for each suffix in suffix array with its predecessor in the suffix array.

The suffix tree is a tree built from all the suffixes of X. Each edge in the suffix tree is labeled by a corresponding substring of X which we call the *edge-label*. Recall that edge-labels are implicit. Each is presented by two position pointers into input string X. Each leaf node represents a suffix from X. For convenience we label it by the suffix start position. The tree contains *internal nodes* and a *leaf nodes*. During the construction we distinguish between *explicit* (already existing) and *implicit* internal nodes. An *implicit node* is a point inside an edge where a new internal node is to be created.

A *path* in the suffix tree connects the root node with any given node and consists of a sequence of symbols on concatenated edge-labels. The *depth* of any node of the suffix tree is the total number of symbols on the path from the root to this node.

2.1   TRANSFORMATION ALGORITHMS

In this section, we show that any of the full-text indexes presented in the previous chapter can be constructed from one another, using an efficient external memory algorithm. To be precise, we need to exclude the plain suffix array (Section 1.2) as it can be converted into a suffix tree only if it is augmented with the LCP array. We remind that each suffix in such an augmented suffix array is represented by two numbers: the start position of this suffix in the input string and the length of the LCP with the previous suffix in the suffix array.

  We begin with a construction of a suffix array SA (and the corresponding LCP array) from a suffix tree ST. We assume that the children of each internal suffix tree node are lexicographically sorted. If we perform a depth-first traversal of the tree, then the leaves of the suffix tree will be accessed in an order that corresponds to the lexicographic ordering of the suffixes that these leaves represent. Thus, the suffix array can be formed from the suffix tree just by performing such a traversal. Visiting of the tree nodes during the depth-first traversal is called an *Euler tour*. Furthermore, if we keep track on the depth of internal nodes visited during the Euler tour, then the internal node of the smallest depth that was visited between two leaves representing suffixes S_i and S_j is called the *lowest common ancestor* of these two suffixes. The depth of this internal node is equal to the $lcp_{i,j}$. The beginning of an Euler tour on the suffix tree for string *ababc* is shown in Figure 2.1. Because

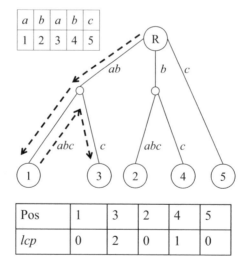

Figure 2.1: Transforming a suffix tree into a suffix array. A part of the depth-first traversal is shown with dotted arrows. The leaves accessed on the Euler tour represent lexicographically sorted suffixes. The internal node of smallest depth, visited between two leaves, represents the lowest common ancestor of the two leaves. It contributes *lcp* values in the *LCP* array.

there are $O(N)$ nodes in a suffix tree, the traversal is performed in linear time. Note, however, that in order to be efficient from the disk-access point of view, the suffix tree should be layered on disk in a manner that permits sequential access to tree nodes during an Euler tour. One of the possibilities is to break the entire tree into a set of subtrees, where each subtree represents suffixes that share some common prefix, and to perform the tour by incrementally loading the subtrees into main memory according to the lexicographic order of these prefixes.

The opposite transformation, constructing suffix tree ST for a given suffix array SA with LCP array, proceeds by inserting the suffixes into the tree in lexicographic order. Specifically, the suffixes are added to the suffix tree from left to right. A new leaf for suffix S_i always becomes a rightmost child of some node v on the rightmost path of the partial suffix tree. We call such a path a *border path*. Furthermore, the *lcp* value in the LCP array tells the depth of v, where the new leaf for S_i is to be added. Consider the example in Figure 2.2. Here, a new leaf for suffix S_3 becomes a rightmost

a	b	a	b	c
1	2	3	4	5

Pos	1	3	2	4	5
lcp	0	2	0	1	0

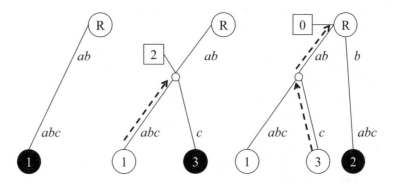

Figure 2.2: Transforming a suffix array into a suffix tree. The place of the internal node where a new leaf is to be created is obtained from its *lcp* value. The nodes on the right-most path (the border path) are accessed in the bottom-up fashion, simulating an Euler tour on the suffix tree under construction. Hence, the conversion of a suffix array into a suffix tree is performed in linear time.

child of some node on the border path. The $lcp_{1,3} = 2$ tells us the depth of this internal node. All the nodes on the border path can be kept in a stack with the leaf node on top. For a new leaf, nodes are popped from the stack until the edge at the corresponding depth is reached. If needed, a new internal node v is created at depth lcp from the root by splitting the found edge. Both the new node and the new leaf are pushed to the stack for subsequent processing.

By inserting in this order and by traversing the border path bottom-up we simulate an Euler tour on the suffix tree nodes. Since such a traversal never accesses the same node of the suffix tree more than twice, the entire conversion of the suffix array into a suffix tree runs in time $O(N)$. This transformation is efficient from a disk-access point of view, since the suffix array is accessed sequentially, and since for a suffix tree we need only keep in memory the stack of the nodes on the border path. All the other nodes can be kept on disk.

We have shown that different forms of full-text indexes (excluding the plain suffix array) are equivalent, namely any of them can be constructed from another by a sequential scan. All we need to do is to be able to efficiently construct one of them from scratch. Next we discuss the construction of a suffix tree directly from input string X.

2.2   BRUTE-FORCE ALGORITHMS

An intuitive method of constructing suffix tree ST is the following: for a given string X we start with a tree consisting of only a root node. We then successively add paths corresponding to each suffix of X, from the longest to the shortest. This results in Algorithm 1. Assume that ST is the partial suffix tree after the insertion of all suffixes up to suffix S_{i-1}. The *update* operation inserts a path corresponding to the next suffix S_i, updating partial tree ST. In order to insert suffix S_i into the tree we first locate some implicit or explicit node corresponding to the longest common prefix of S_i with some other suffix already in the tree. To locate this node, we perform lcp character comparisons. After this, if the path ends in an implicit internal node, it is transformed into an explicit internal node. In any case, we add to this internal node a new leaf corresponding to suffix S_i. Once the location of the insertion point is found, we add a new child in constant time. Finding the end of the LCP for the current suffix S_i in the tree defines the overall time complexity of the algorithm. The end of the LCP can be found in one step in the best case but in the worst case in N steps for each of the N inserted suffixes. This leads to $O(N^2)$ total character comparisons.

Algorithm 1: Brute-force suffix tree construction.

---

    input : string X of length N
    output: suffix tree ST of X

1 initialize ST with the empty root node;
2 **for** $i = 1, \cdots, N$ **do**
3 | ST=update(ST, S_i);
4 **end**
5 **return** ST;

Nevertheless, based on this brute-force approach, the Hunt algorithm – the first practical external memory suffix tree construction algorithm – was developed. Hunt's incremental construction has good locality of access to the tree during its construction. The output tree is represented as a

---

Function update(ST, S_i)

    input : partial tree ST, current suffix S_i

    output: modified tree ST

1 match lcp characters of S_i to the path in ST starting from the root;

2 **if** *the path ends in explicit node* **then**

3 | add child leaf labeled by $X[i + lcp + 1, N]$;

4 **end**

5 **else**

6 | create explicit node at depth lcp from the root;

7 | add child leaf labeled by $X[i + lcp + 1, N]$;

8 **end**

9 **return** ST;

---

forest of several suffix trees. The suffixes in each such tree share a common prefix. Each tree is built independently and requires scanning of the entire input string for each such prefix. The idea is that suffixes that have prefix, say, *aa* fall into a different subtree than those starting with *ab*, *ac* and *ad*. Hence, once the tree for all suffixes starting with *aa* is built, it is never accessed again. The tree for each prefix is constructed independently in main memory. Then it is written to disk. The disk-optimized modification of Algorithm 1 results in Algorithm 2.

The number of partitions p is computed as the ratio of the space required for the tree of the entire input string, $|ST_{total}|$, to the size of the available main memory M, i.e., $p = |ST_{total}|/M$. Then, if the number of suffixes in each partition is the same, the length of the prefix for each partition can be computed as $\log_{|\Sigma|} p$, where $|\Sigma|$ is the size of the alphabet. This is true because we need to obtain p total prefixes of equal size by creating p permutations of all available characters. For example, if $\Sigma = \{a, b, c, d\}$, and we want to generate 16 equal partitions, the prefix for each partition would contain $\log_4 16 = 2$ characters. Note that the number of partitions grows exponentially on the prefix length. This partitioning scheme works well for non-skewed input data but fails when there is a significantly larger amount of suffixes for a particular prefix. This is often the case in DNA sequences with a large amount of repetitive substrings. In order to fit a tree for each possible prefix into main memory, we can increase the length of the prefix. This, in turn, exponentially increases the total number of partitions and, therefore, the total number of input string scans.

The construction of the sub-tree for prefix *ab* and input string $X = ababcababd$ is shown in Figure 2.3. Note that each sub-tree is significantly smaller than the suffix tree for the entire input string.

We remark that we iterate through the input string as many times as the total number of partitions. The construction of a tree for each partition is performed in main memory. At the end, the suffix tree for each partition is written to disk. Note also that in order to perform the brute-force insertion of each suffix into the tree, we need to randomly access the input string X, which therefore

---

Algorithm 2: The algorithm by Hunt.

---

input : string X of length N, main memory size M
output: forest of suffix trees ST_j ($1 \leq j \leq p$) of X on disk

1 compute total number of prefixes p such that each suffix tree for all suffixes with prefix P_i fits M;
2 **for** $j = 1, \cdots, p$ **do**
3   initialize ST_j for prefix P_j with the empty root node;
4   **for** $i = 1, \cdots, N$ **do**
5   ST_j=updatePrefixedSubtree(ST_j, S_i, P_j);
6   **end**
7   write ST_j to disk;
8 **end**

Function updatePrefixedSubtree(ST_j, S_i, P_j)

---

input : partial tree ST_j, current suffix S_i, current prefix P_j
output: modified tree ST_j

1 **if** S_i *begins with prefix* P_j **then**
2   match lcp characters of S_i to the path in ST_j starting from the root;
3   **if** *the path ends in explicit node* **then**
4   add child leaf labeled by $X[i + lcp + 1, N]$;
5   **end**
6   **else**
7   create explicit node at depth lcp from the root;
8   add child leaf labeled by $X[i + lcp + 1, N]$;
9   **end**
10   **return** ST_j;
11 **end**

---

has to reside in memory. Since the input string is at least an order of magnitude smaller than the tree, this method efficiently addresses the problem of random accesses to the tree in secondary storage, but cannot be extended to inputs that are larger than the main-memory allocated for X.

2.3 ALGORITHMS BASED ON SUFFIX-LINKS

We start by describing the linear-time construction algorithm by Ukkonen that works well in main memory, but cannot be successfully extended to a disk version. This algorithm assumes that random access to the input string and to the tree takes constant time. Unfortunately, in practice, when some

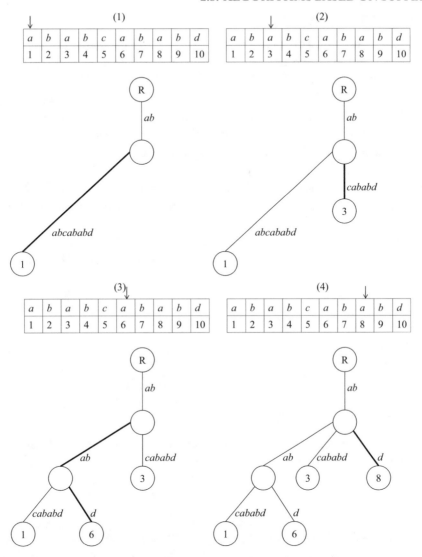

Figure 2.3: The steps of building the sub-tree for prefix *ab* and input string $X = ababcababd$ with the Hunt algorithm.

of these data structures outgrow the main memory and are accessed directly on disk, the access time to disk-based arrays varies significantly depending on the relative location of the data on disk. The total number of random disk accesses for this algorithm is, in fact, $O(N)$. This presents a significant challenge for large values of N.

2.3.1   THE UKKONEN ALGORITHM

For a given string X, we start with an empty tree (that is, a tree consisting just of a root node) and then progressively build an intermediate suffix tree ST_i for each prefix $P_i = X[1, i]$, $1 \leq i \leq N$. In order to convert a suffix tree ST_{i-1} into ST_i, each suffix of ST_{i-1} is extended with the next character x_i. We do this by visiting each suffix of ST_{i-1} in order, starting with the longest suffix and ending with the shortest one (empty string). The suffixes inserted into ST_{i-1} may end in three types of nodes: leaf nodes, internal nodes or in the middle of an edge (at a so-called *implicit* internal node). Note that if a suffix of ST_{i-1} ends in a leaf node, we do not need to extend it with the next character. Instead, we consider each leaf node as an open node: at each step of the algorithm every leaf node runs till the end of the current prefix, meaning the end position on each leaf node will eventually become N. Consider an example in Figure 2.4. It shows the three first iterations of the suffix tree

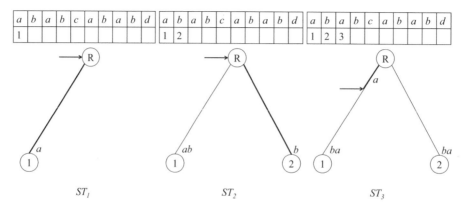

Figure 2.4: The three first steps of the Ukkonen algorithm. An arrow indicates the active point at the end of each iteration. Note that the extension of the edges ending at leaf nodes with the next character is performed implicitly: the edge length is just extended by 1.

construction for $X = ababcababd$. In the second iteration, we implicitly extend the a-child of a root node with b, and we add a new edge for b from the root (extending an empty suffix).

Thus, in each iteration, we need to update only suffixes of ST_{i-1} that end at explicit or implicit internal nodes of ST_{i-1}. We find the end of the longest among such suffixes at the *active point*. The active point is the (explicit or implicit) internal node where the previous iteration ended. If the node at the active point already has a child starting with x_i, the active point advances one position down the corresponding edge. This means that all the suffixes of ST_i already exist in ST_{i-1} as the prefixes of some other suffixes. In case that there is no outgoing edge starting with the new character, we add a new leaf node as a child of our explicit or implicit internal node (active point). Here, an implicit internal node becomes explicit. In order to move to the extension of the next suffix, which is shorter by one character, we follow the chain of *suffix links*. A suffix link is a directed edge from each internal node of the suffix tree (source) to some other internal node whose incoming path is one (the first)

Algorithm 3: The algorithm by Ukkonen.

input : string X of length N
output: suffix tree ST of X

1 initialize ST with the empty root node;
2 initialize $activePoint$=root;
3 **for** $i = 1, \cdots , N$ **do**
4 | ST=updateTree(ST *with activePoint, prefix* P_i);
5 **end**
6 **return** ST;

---

character shorter than the incoming path of the source node. The suffix links are added when the sequence of internal nodes is created during edge splits.

To illustrate, consider the last iteration of the Ukkonen algorithm – extending an intermediate tree for $X = ababcababd$ with the last character d. We extend all the suffixes of ST_9 (Figure 2.5 (1)) with this last character. The active point is originally two characters below the node labeled by $\star$ in Figure 2.5 (1), and the implicit internal node is indicated by an arrow. The active point is converted to an explicit internal node with two children: one of them is the existing leaf with edge label $cababd$ and the other one is a new leaf for suffix S_6 (Figure 2.5 (2)). Then, we follow the suffix link from the $\star$-node to the $\star\star$-node, and we add a new leaf by splitting an implicit node two characters below the $\star\star$-node. This results in the tree of Figure 2.5 (3) with a leaf for suffix S_7. Next, the suffix link from the $\star\star$-node leads us to the root node. Two characters along the corresponding edge we find the $\star$-node and add to it a new edge starting with d, leading to a leaf node for suffix S_8 (Figure 2.5 (4)). We continue in a similar manner and add the corresponding child starting with d both to the $\star\star$-node (Figure 2.5 (5)) and to the root (Figure 2.5 (6)). This illustrates how suffix links help to find all the insertion points for new leaf nodes. There is a constant number of steps per leaf creation; therefore, the total amortized running time of the Ukkonen algorithm is $O(N)$.

Algorithm 3 and function *updateTree* present a basic pseudocode of the Ukkonen algorithm. Each call to *updateTree* converts ST_{i-1} into ST_i. The call to *NextSmallerSuffix* (line 29) finds the next suffix by following a suffix link.

If we look at Algorithm 3 from the disk access point of view, we see that locating the next suffix requires a random tree traversal, one per created leaf. Hence, when tree ST_{i-1} is to be stored on disk, a node access requires an entire random disk I/O. This access time depends on the location on disk of the next access point. Moreover, since the edges of the tree are not labeled with actual characters, it is important that we access randomly the input string in order to compare the current character with the characters of X encoded as positions in the suffix tree edges. Unfortunately, this leads to a very impractical performance since the algorithm spends all its time moving the disk head from one random disk location to another.

Function updateTree(ST, P_i)

---

input : tree ST for prefix P_{i-1} with *activePoint*, current prefix P_i
output: tree ST for prefix P_i

1 *currentSufEnd = activePoint*;
2 *currentChar = X[i]*;
3 *done*=false;
4 **while** *not done* **do**
5   **if** *currentSufEnd is at explicit node v* **then**
6   **if** *v has no child starting with currentChar* **then**
7   create new leaf;
8   **end**
9   **else**
10   advance *activePoint* down the corresponding edge;
11   *done* = true;
12   **end**
13   **end**
14   **else**
15   **if** *the implicit node's next char is not equal currentChar* **then**
16   create new explicit node;
17   create new leaf;
18   **end**
19   **else**
20   advance *activePoint* down the corresponding edge;
21   *done* = true;
22   **end**
23   **end**
24   **if** *currentSufEnd is at root* **then**
25   *done* = true;
26   **end**
27   **else**
28   proceed to the next smaller suffix following a suffix link ;
29   *currentSufEnd* = NextSmallerSuffix ;
30   **end**
31 **end**
32 *activePoint = currentSufEnd*;
33 **return** ST;

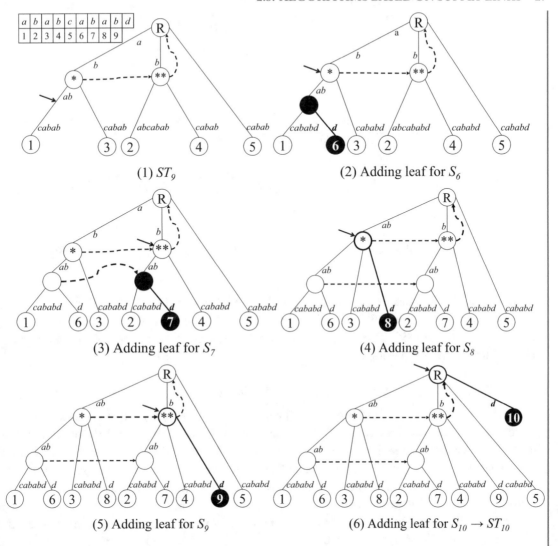

Figure 2.5: The last steps of the Ukkonen algorithm applied to $X = ababcababd$. In this cascade of leaf additions ST_9 is updated to ST_{10}. The place for the next insertion is found following the suffix links (dotted arrows).

The access can be optimized. The higher tree nodes are accessed much more frequently than the deeper ones. This gave rise to the buffer management method known as *TOP-Q*. In this on-disk version of Ukkonen's algorithm, nodes that are accessed often have a priority of staying in the memory buffer, while the other nodes are eventually read from disk. This significantly improves the

a	b	a	b	c	a	b	a	b	d	a	b	a	b	e
1	2	3	4	5	6	7	8	9	10	11	12	13	14	15

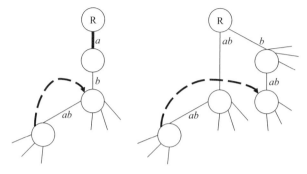

Figure 2.6:   Difference between sparse suffix links **[Left]** and traditional suffix links **[Right]**.

hit rate for accessed nodes when compared to rather straightforward implementations. However, in practical terms, in order to build the suffix tree for the DNA sequence of the Human chromosome I (approximately 247 MB), *TOP-Q* runs for hundreds of hours and cannot be considered a practical method for indexing larger inputs.

2.3.2   DISTRIBUTED AND PAGED SUFFIX TREES

An idea of using suffix links but processing the suffixes of X separately for each prefix resulted in the distributed and paged suffix tree (*DPST*) algorithm. As in the Hunt algorithm, the suffixes of X are grouped by their common prefix whose length depends on the size N of X and the amount of the available main memory. The number of suffixes in each subtree is small enough for the tree to be entirely built in main memory. Therefore, random disk access to the sub-tree during its construction is avoided. The main difference from Hunt's algorithm of Section 2.2 is that the sub-tree for each particular prefix is built in an asymptotic time *linear* in N and not quadratic. In order to do so, the *DPST* algorithm uses ideas similar to the Ukkonen algorithm described in Section 2.3.1. However, the Ukkonen algorithm relies heavily on the fact that *all* suffixes of X are inserted in sequence, whereas each sub-tree is built only for some suffixes of X, namely the ones that share the particular prefix.

   DPST introduces the idea of *sparse suffix links* (SSL) instead of regular suffix links. A SSL in a particular subtree leads from each internal node v_i with incoming path label w to another internal node v_j in the same sub-tree whose incoming path-label corresponds to the largest possible suffix of w found in the same sub-tree (or to the root if the largest such suffix is an empty string).

   We explain the difference between a sparse suffix link and a regular suffix link in the following example. Suppose we have a sub-tree for a prefix a of $X = ababcababdababe$ (see Figure 2.6). In the regular suffix tree, the suffix link from the internal node with edge label *abab* leads to the node with edge label *bab*. However, in the sub-tree for prefix *a*, there is no suffix starting with *bab*. Thus, the longest suffix of *abab* that can be found in this sub-tree is *ab*, and the SSL leads to the internal node with edge label *ab*.

Let us follow an example of the sub-tree construction for $X = ababcababdababe$ and prefix *a* in Figure 2.7. This sub-tree will contain only the suffixes of X starting at positions 1, 3, 6, 8, 11, 13.

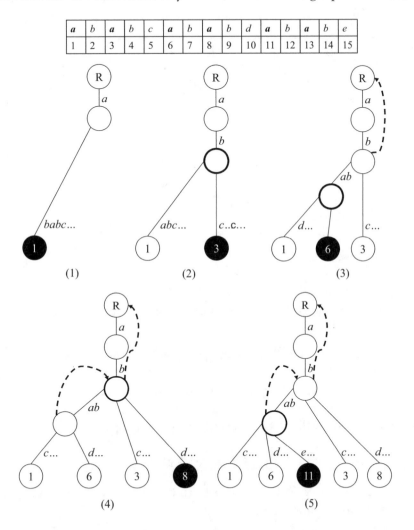

Figure 2.7: Steps of the construction of the sub-tree for prefix *a* by the distributed and paged suffix tree (DPST) construction algorithm for input string $X = ababcababdababe$.

Thus, we need to insert only these six suffixes into the tree. First, we insert suffix S_1 by creating the corresponding leaf (Figure 2.7 (1)). Next, we add S_3 by finding that $x_2 = x_4$ and $x_3 \neq x_5$. We split an edge and add a leaf for S_3 (Figure 2.7 (2)). Now it is the turn for suffix S_6. The first four characters of S_6 correspond to some path in the tree, but $x_{10} = d$ does not. Therefore, we add a leaf for S_6 and create an internal node with incoming path label *abab*. We see that the longest suffix of *abab* in this sub-tree is *ab*. We create a sparse suffix link from the internal node for *abab* (marked by ⋆⋆ in Figure 2.8) to the one for *ab* (marked by ⋆). When we create a new leaf out of the ⋆⋆-node for suffix S_{11}, we follow the SSL and create the same *e*-child from the ⋆-node (Figure 2.8 (5)).

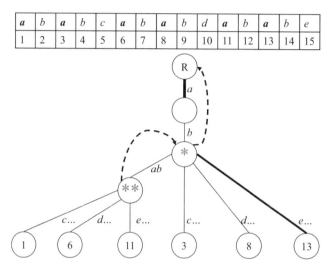

Figure 2.8:   Sample output of the *DPST* algorithm: each suffix sub-tree contains sparse suffix links.

The use of sparse suffix links when adding new leaves to the sub-tree allows to perform the construction of each sub-tree in time linear in N. $DPST$ runs in time $O(Np)$ where p is the total number of different prefixes. Despite the superior asymptotic internal running time w.r.t. the previous brute-force algorithm, there was no significant improvement in performance, because the running time is dominated by disk I/Os and not by in-memory operations.

2.4   DISK-OPTIMIZED ALGORITHMS

In this section we describe three suffix tree construction algorithms that were designed to further reduce random access to the suffix tree being built.

2.4.1   THE TOP DOWN ALGORITHM

An elaborated approach of the Top Down Disk based suffix tree construction algorithm (*TDD*) takes the performance of the on-disk suffix tree construction to the next level. Being still an $O(N^2)$ approach, *TDD* manages the memory buffers more efficiently and it is a cache-conscious method, which performs very well for many practical inputs.

The first step of *TDD* is the partitioning of the input string in a way similar to that of the algorithm by Hunt. Now, the tree for each partition is built as follows. The suffixes of each partition are first collected into an array where they are represented by their start positions. Next, the suffixes are grouped by their first character into *character groups*. The number of different character groups corresponds to the number of children for the current tree node. If for some character there is a group consisting only of one suffix, then this is a leaf node and is immediately written to the tree (disk). If there is more than one suffix in the group, the *lcp* value of all the suffixes is computed by sequential scans of X from different random positions. An internal node at the corresponding depth is written to the tree. After advancing the position of each suffix by *lcp*, the same procedure as before is repeated recursively. The pseudocode of the *TDD* algorithm is given in Algorithm 4.

Algorithm 4: The *TDD* algorithm.

---

    input : string X of length N
    output: forest of suffix trees ST_j $(1 \leq j \leq p)$ of X on disk

1 create collection $\mathcal{P}$ of p equal-sized prefixes;
2 **foreach** P_j *in* $\mathcal{P}$ **do**
3   initialize ST_j for prefix P_j with the empty root node;
4   collect start positions of suffixes starting with P_j into array;
5   advance each start position by $|P_j|$;
6   assign suffixes to one of at most Σ character groups according to the first character;
7   output to disk groups with 1 suffix as leaf nodes of ST_j;
8   push groups with more than 1 suffix into *stack*;
9   **while** *stack is not empty* **do**
10   pop suffix group from *stack*;
11   compute *lcp* for all suffixes in this group by sequential scan;
12   output to disk internal node of ST_j at depth *lcp*;
13   advance position of each suffix by *lcp*;
14   assign suffixes to one of new character groups according to the first character;
15   output to disk new groups with 1 suffix as leaf nodes of ST_j;
16   push new groups with more than 1 suffix into the stack;
17   **end**
18 **end**

To illustrate the algorithm, let us observe several steps of the *TDD* suffix tree construction, which are depicted in Figure 2.9. Suppose that we have partitioned all the suffixes of X by a prefix of length 1. This results in four partitions: a, b, c and d. We show how *TDD* builds the suffix tree for partition b. The start positions of suffixes starting with b are $\{2, 4, 7, 9\}$. Since the prefix length is 1, the characters at positions $\{3, 5, 8, 10\}$ are sorted lexicographically (Figure 2.9 (1)). This produces three groups of suffixes: a-group: $\{3, 8\}$, c-group: $\{5\}$ and d-group: $\{10\}$. Since the c-group and the

d-group contain one suffix each, the suffixes in these groups produce leaf nodes and are immediately added to the tree (Figure 2.9 (1)). The a-group contains two suffixes, and is therefore a branching node. $lcp_{3,8} = 2$, and therefore the length of the child starting with a equals 2. At this depth, the internal node (Figure 2.9 (2)) branches at positions {5, 10}. After sorting, this results into two leaf nodes: the children starting with c and d, respectively, (Figure 2.9 (3)).

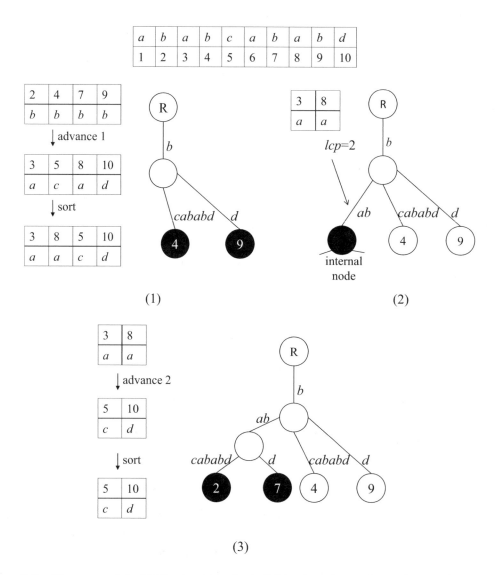

Figure 2.9: The steps of the TDD algorithm for building the sub-tree for prefix b and input string $X = ababcababd$.

The main distinctive feature of the *TDD* construction is the order in which the tree nodes are added to the output tree. Observe that the tree is written in a top-down fashion, and that the nodes that were expanded in the current iteration are not accessed anymore. This reduces the number of random accesses to the partially built tree and the new nodes can be written directly to the disk. The number of random disk accesses is $O(p)$ as in Hunt et al.'s algorithm. However, the size of each partition may be much bigger than before since now the main memory buffer for the suffix tree data structure does not have to hold an entire sub-tree.

This pattern of accessing the tree was shown to be very efficient for cached architectures of modern machines. It was even shown that the *TDD* algorithm outperforms the linear-time algorithm by Ukkonen for some inputs in the case where all the data structures fit the main memory. We remind that the reason for this is that the completely random access to main memory is slower than the sequential access to modern disks (see diagram in Figure 1.13). For the same input of 250 millions of symbols (Human chromosome I), it takes 100 hours to construct the suffix tree using the optimized Ukkonen algorithm, about 1.5 hours using the suffix-by-suffix insertion of Hunt, while *TDD* builds the tree in 20 minutes.

As before, the algorithm performs massive random accesses to the input string when it does the character-by-character comparisons starting at different random positions. The input string for the *TDD* algorithm cannot be larger than the main memory.

Another problem of *TDD* is the suffix tree on-disk layout. The trees for different partitions are of different sizes, and some of them can be significantly larger than the main memory. This poses some problems when loading the subtree into main memory for querying. If the entire subtree cannot be loaded into and traversed in the main memory, the depth first traversal of such a tree requires multiple random accesses to different levels of on-disk nodes.

2.4.2   THE PARTITION-AND-MERGE ALGORITHM

Oversized subtrees caused by data skew can be eliminated by using a set of variable-length prefixes. In practice, the initial prefix size is chosen so that the total number of prefixes p will allow to process each of the p sub-trees in main memory. For example, we can hold in our main memory in total T_{max} suffix tree nodes. The counts in each group of suffixes sharing the same prefix are computed by a sequential scan of input string X. If a count exceeds T_{max}, then we re-scan the input string from the beginning, collecting counters for an increased prefix length. Based on the final counts, none of which exceeds T_{max}, the suffixes are combined into approximately even-sized groups. As an example consider the case when suffixes starting with prefix *ab* occur twice more often than the suffixes starting with *ba* and *bb*. We can combine suffixes in partitions *ba* and *bb* into a single partition *b* with approximately the same number of suffixes as contained in partition *ab*. The maximum number of suffixes in each prefix partition is chosen to ensure that the size of the tree for suffixes which share the same prefix will never exceed the main memory. This is done in order to ensure that each such subtree can be built and queried in main memory.

This new partitioning scheme was used in the *Trellis*[1] algorithm. The main innovative idea of this method is the combination of the prefix partitioning and the horizontal partitioning of the input into consecutive substrings, or *chunks*. In theory, the substring partitioning does not work for any input, since the suffixes in each substring partition do not run until the end of the entire input string. However, this horizontal partitioning works for most practical inputs. Consider, for example, the Human genome – a DNA sequence of about 3 GB in length. In fact, there is not a single string representing Human genome, but rather 23 sequences of DNA in 23 different Human chromosomes, with the largest sequence being only about 247 MB in size. Those chromosome sequences represent natural partitions of the entire genome.

If the size of each natural chunk of the input does not allow us to build the suffix tree for it entirely in main-memory, then the chunk can be split into several slightly overlapping substrings. We append to the end of each such substring except the last one, a small "tail" – the prefix of the next partition. The tail of the partition must never occur as a substring of this partition. It serves as a sentinel for the suffixes of the partition, and its positions are not included into the suffix tree of the partition. In practice, for most real-life sequences, the length of such a tail is negligibly small compared to the size of the partition itself.

After partitioning the input into chunks of appropriate size, *Trellis* builds an independent suffix tree for each chunk. It does not output the entire suffix tree to disk, but rather writes to disk the different sub-trees of the in-memory tree. These sub-trees correspond to the different variable-length prefixes. Once trees for each chunk are built and written to disk, *Trellis* loads into memory the subtrees for all the chunks that share the same prefix. Then it merges these subtrees into the shared-prefix-based subtree for an entire input string. The pseudocode of the *Trellis* algorithm is shown in Algorithm 5.

As an example, let us apply the *Trellis* method to our input string $X = ababcababd$. Let the collection of prefixes for a prefix-based partitioning be $\{ab, ba, c, d\}$. We partition X into two substrings $X_1 = abab$ with "tail" c and $X_2 = cababd$. Note the overlapping symbol c that is used as a sentinel for suffixes of X_1. We build in memory the suffix tree for X_1, shown in Figure 2.10 (1), and output it to disk in the form of two different subtrees: one for prefix ab and the second for prefix ba. The same procedure is performed for X_2 (Figure 2.10 (2)). Then, we load into main memory the subtrees for, say, prefix ab and we merge those sub-trees into the common ab-subtree for the entire X.

The merge of subtrees for different chunks is performed by a straightforward character-by-character comparison, which leads to the same $O(N^2)$ worst-case number of character comparisons as the brute force algorithms described before. If we have k chunks and p prefixes in the variable-length prefixes collection, the number of random disk accesses is $O(kp)$. Since both k and p depend on the length of the input string N, the execution time of *Trellis* grows quadratically with the increase of N. During the character-by-character comparison in the merge step, the input string is randomly

---

[1]*Trellis* stands for **E**xternal **S**uffix **TR**ee with Suffix **L**inks for **I**ndexing Genome-Sca**L**e **S**equences.

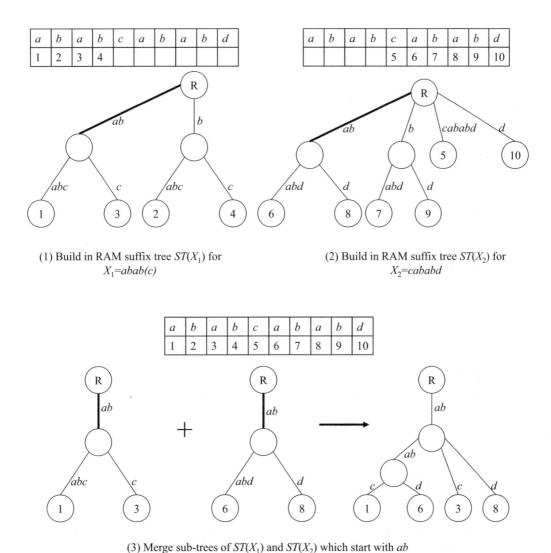

(1) Build in RAM suffix tree $ST(X_1)$ for
$X_1=abab(c)$

(2) Build in RAM suffix tree $ST(X_2)$ for
$X_2=cababd$

(3) Merge sub-trees of $ST(X_1)$ and $ST(X_2)$ which start with ab

Figure 2.10: The steps of the *Trellis* algorithm applied to input string $X = ababcababd$. (1). Building the suffix tree for substring $X_1 = abab(c)$. (2). Building the suffix tree for substring $X_2 = cababd$. (3). Merging the sub-trees for prefix ab. The total size of the tree structures at each step allows to perform each step in main memory.

Algorithm 5: The *Trellis* algorithm.

---

input : string X of length N

output: forest of suffix trees ST_j ($1 \leq j \leq p$) of X on disk

1 partition X into k substrings $X_1, \cdots, X_k$ such that suffix tree for each substring fits in RAM;

2 create collection $\mathcal{P}$ of p variable-sized prefixes;

3 **for** $j = 1, \cdots, k$ **do**

4   build suffix tree $ST(X_j)$ by Ukkonen algorithm (see Algorithm 3);

5   **foreach** P_j *in* $\mathcal{P}$ **do**

6   find in $ST(X_j)$ the sub-tree starting with P_j;

7   write this sub-tree into a separate file on disk;

8   **end**

9 **end**

10 **foreach** P_j *in* $\mathcal{P}$ **do**

11   load from disk into RAM all sub-trees starting with P_j;

12   merge sub-trees into 1 sub-tree for prefix P_j;

13   write the full sub-tree for P_j back to disk;

14 **end**

---

accessed at different positions all over the input string. Therefore, the scalability of *Trellis* does not go beyond the size of the main memory designated for the input.

2.4.3 THE MERGE SORT ALGORITHM

Another simple but powerful approach to construct suffix trees on disk is based on external memory multi-way merge sort. The *DiGeST*[2] algorithm scales for larger inputs since it does not use the prefix-based partitioning, but rather outputs a collection of small suffix trees for the different sorted lexicographic intervals.

    The main ideas of *DiGeST* are based on the following observation. The locality of references during the suffix tree construction can be significantly improved if we insert *sorted* suffixes into the suffix tree. In this case, if we collect and write to disk the suffix tree for all suffixes in a given lexicographic interval, then we do not access the completed part of the tree anymore. Thus, the first step is to obtain an array of lexicographically sorted suffixes, a *suffix array*.

    Once we obtain an array of lexicographically sorted suffixes, we can insert each suffix into a growing suffix tree. In order to insert the next suffix, one internal node is created at depth lcp from the root of the suffix tree, and a new leaf is added. This process is performed in main memory. Once

---

[2] *DiGeST* stands for **Di**sk-based **Ge**neralized **S**uffix **T**ree.

the suffix tree for a given lexicographic interval is complete, it is written to disk and never accessed again.

The efficient external memory sorting of suffixes is based on the paradigm of two-phase multi-way merge-sort. Conventional multi-way merge sort works as follows. It partitions an input array of values into k sub-arrays. The size of each sub-array is bounded by the available main memory. In the first phase, the algorithm sorts the elements of each sub-array (using any efficient main-memory sorting algorithm). The sorted sub-arrays, called *runs*, are written to disk. The main idea of multi-way merging is to merge the sorted lists from multiple runs at the same time. The algorithm allocates k input buffers, one input buffer for each active (unfinished) run, and one output buffer. Each buffer has a pointer to the next element of the corresponding run. Then, all the currently pointed values of each run are compared, and the smallest (belonging to a buffer, say, i) is transferred to an output buffer. The pointer in buffer i is advanced by 1. If buffer i is now exhausted of elements, we read the next blocks from the corresponding run. Once no data remains in that run, it is considered no longer active. When the output buffer is full, it is written to the end of the output file. When only one active run remains, the algorithm finishes up by copying all the remaining elements to the end of the output file.

A similar merge-sort approach is used for *DiGeST*. Recall that unlike the conventional sort applied to numbers or short strings, we are sorting suffixes, which are long overlapping strings. This, in general, requires special sorting and merging techniques developed for suffix sorting. However, in the suffix merge step *DiGeST* performs a direct character-by-character comparison of suffixes from different partitions, trading the efficiency of suffix sorting for a better pattern of random disk I/Os.

To perform multi-way merge sort, *DiGeST* first partitions the input string into k chunks. The suffixes in each chunk are sorted using any in-memory suffix sorting algorithm. The suffix array for each chunk is written to disk. To each position in this suffix array a short prefix of the suffix is attached. These prefixes significantly improve the performance of the merging phase.

After sorting the suffixes in each chunk, consecutive pieces of each of the k suffix arrays are read from the disk into input buffers. As in the regular multi-way merge sort, a "competition" is run among the top elements of each buffer and the "winning" suffix migrates to an output buffer organized as a suffix tree. When the output buffer is full, it is emptied to disk. In order to determine the order of suffixes from different input chunks, we first compare the prefixes attached to each suffix start position. Only if these prefixes are equal, we compare the rest of the suffixes character-by-character. This comparison incurs random access to the input string, and therefore it requires that the input string be kept in main memory.

Due to the character-by-character comparison of the suffixes, *DiGeST* runs in $O(N^2)$ internal time. The same comparison is performed in order to calculate the longest common prefix of the current suffix with the last suffix previously inserted into the tree. The calculated lcp determines the place where the internal node is created, and a new leaf for each suffix is added as a child of this internal node. This way we build the suffix tree in the output buffer.

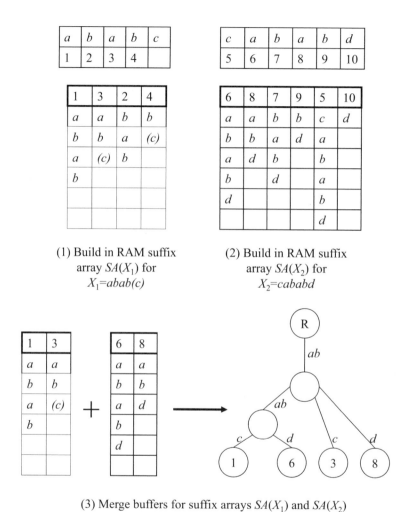

(1) Build in RAM suffix
array $SA(X_1)$ for
$X_1 = abab(c)$

(2) Build in RAM suffix
array $SA(X_2)$ for
$X_2 = cababd$

(3) Merge buffers for suffix arrays $SA(X_1)$ and $SA(X_2)$
into ST_1 for interval from aba to abd

Figure 2.11: The steps of the *DiGeST* algorithm applied to input string $X = ababcababd$. (1). Building the suffix array for substring $X_1 = abab(c)$. (2). Building the suffix array for substring $X_2 = cababd$. (3). Merging the suffix arrays by uploading them sequentially from disk. Once the output suffix tree fills the entire output buffer, it is written to disk as a sub-tree corresponding to a particular lexicographic interval.

Before writing the output buffer to disk, the lexicographically largest suffix in this tree is added to a collection of "dividers" which serve locating multiple trees on disk. Since the output buffer is of a pre-calculated size, all trees are of equal size, and thus, the problem of data skew is completely avoided. Further, each tree is small enough to be quickly loaded into the main memory to perform a search or comparative analysis. The pseudocode of *DiGeST* is presented in Algorithm 6.

Algorithm 6: The *Digest* algorithm.

    input : string X of length N

    output: forest of suffix trees of X on disk, divided by lexicographic intervals

1 partition X into k substrings $X_1, \cdots, X_k$ such that suffix array for each substring fits in RAM;
2 **for** $j = 1, \cdots, k$ **do**
3   build plain suffix array $SA(X_j)$;
4   write $SA(X_j)$ into a separate file on disk;
5 **end**
6 mergePartitions()

While *DiGeST* still requires the input string to be in main memory, from an external memory point of view it is very efficient: the algorithm performs only two scans over the disk data and, furthermore, accesses the disk mainly sequentially.

2.5   SUMMARY

In this chapter, we presented the state-of-the-art algorithms for the construction of suffix trees on disk. The best performing algorithms – *TDD*, *Trellis* and *DiGeST* – are designed to access the suffix tree sequentially. This allows to keep the suffix tree on disk during its construction. In fact, these algorithms do not produce a complete suffix tree for the input string X, but rather they build a forest of small suffix trees. Each small tree in this forest is identified by a prefix that all its suffixes share, or by a lexicographic interval to which all its suffixes belong. To perform traversals efficiently, the tree should be small enough in order to load it entirely into RAM, since traversals on disk would incur massive random I/Os.

Unfortunately, the scalability of all the presented algorithms does not go beyond input strings that fit the main memory because all the algorithms perform reading characters of the input string from random locations. Suffix tree construction for larger strings is the topic of the next chapter.

2.6   BIBLIOGRAPHIC NOTES

The transformation algorithms are described in Meyer et al. [2003].

The brute-force algorithm for suffix tree construction was adapted to disk settings by Hunt et al. [2001]. Apostolico and Szpankowski [1992] have shown that, on average, the brute-

---

Function mergePartitions

---

    input : k suffix arrays $SA(X_j)$ for sub-strings of X on disk
    output: forest of suffix trees of X on disk, divided by lexicographic intervals

1 allocate k input buffers and 1 output buffer in form of a suffix tree ST_i;
2 **for** $j = 1, \cdots, K$ **do**
3   read part of $SA(X_j)$ from disk into buffer j;
4 **end**
5 create *heap* of size k;
6 read first element of each input buffer into *heap*;
7 **while** *heap is not empty* **do**
8   pop the smallest suffix S_k of X_j from the top of *heap* into output buffer;
9   find *lcp* of this suffix with the last inserted suffix;
10   add to ST_i an internal node at depth *lcp* and a leaf node for suffix S_k;
11   **if** *output buffer is full* **then**
12   record the smallest and the largest suffix in ST_i;
13   write ST_i to disk;
14   initialize a new tree ST_{i+1};
15   **end**
16   **if** *input buffer j is empty and not the end of $SA(X_j)$* **then**
17   fill input buffer j with the next suffixes;
18   **end**
19   **if** *input buffer j is not empty* **then**
20   insert next suffix S_m from input buffer j into *heap*;
21   **end**
22 **end**

---

force construction requires $O(N \log N)$ time. Their analysis was based on the assumption that the symbols of X are independent and randomly selected from an alphabet according to a given probability distribution.

Linear-time algorithms for suffix tree construction in RAM were developed by Weiner [1973], McCreight [1976], and Ukkonen [1995]. Giegerich and Kurtz [1997] have shown that all the three are based on similar algorithmic ideas. The poor locality of accesses in these algorithms let Navarro and Baeza-Yates [2000] to conclude that the suffix tree in secondary storage is inviable. The improvement of the random access behavior of these algorithms was studied by Bedathur and Haritsa [2004], who proposed the TOP-Q algorithm. A combination of the Ukkonen algorithm and Hunt's idea of processing suffixes of X separately for each prefix resulted in the Distributed and Paged construction proposed by Clifford and Sergot [2003].

The Top Down Disk based suffix tree construction algorithm *TDD* was introduced in Tian et al. [2007]. The base of the method is the combination of the *wot-
deager* algorithm of Giegerich et al. [2003] and Hunt et al.'s prefix partitioning described
above. Phoophakdee and Zaki [2007] proposed the *Trellis* partition-and-merge method. The *Di-
GeST* algorithm that performs essentially the multi-way merge-sort of suffixes was proposed
by Barsky et al. [2008].

CHAPTER 3

Scaling Up: When the Input Exceeds the Main Memory

All the suffix tree construction algorithms described so far reduce random access to the suffix tree. Once the input string outgrows the main memory, these algorithms suffer severe performance degradation. The reason for this is that, by design, they assume that massive random access to the input string is performed in RAM. Once the input string is on disk, this translates into a prohibitive number of random disk I/Os. As experiments show, the construction of suffix trees using these algorithms for inputs that are just slightly larger than the main memory may take weeks or months.

The problem of efficiently constructing suffix trees for very large strings is *particularly* important when the input string does not fit in main memory. This is, because if the entire input string is in main memory, then one might be able to find efficient algorithms that scan and search the string without using a (disk-based) index. In such a case, the overhead of constructing and handling the index may not pay off. Therefore, for strings that do not fit in main memory such an index will be the most beneficial.

The problem is difficult, because we need to randomly access the input string many times during the construction of the edges of the suffix tree. Recall that the edges of the suffix tree are not explicitly labeled with the actual, corresponding, substrings, but instead contain pointers to the input string. Hence, if an algorithm requires a comparison of the characters in the input string with the characters of an edge-label, we inevitably need to access the input string at multiple arbitrary locations.

In the following, we present two algorithms that are specifically designed to handle inputs in excess of RAM. First, in Section 3.1, we present an algorithm that performs a tiled construction of suffix trees. Next, in Section 3.2, we present an extension of multi-way merge sort for the case of oversized inputs, based on pairwise partition sorting. These algorithms are able to handle inputs several times larger than main memory.

3.1 THE WAVEFRONT ALGORITHM

The *Wavefront* algorithm is designed to build a suffix tree by keeping the input string on disk, and by performing numerous sequential scans on it. Despite the multiple scans, this algorithm performs better for oversized strings than any algorithm described so far, because of the limiting factor inherent in all the previous algorithms, namely the number of *random* disk I/Os to the input string. The pseudocode of *Wavefront* is given in Algorithm 7.

Algorithm 7: The *Wavefront* algorithm.

---

   input : string X of length N on disk;
   b - size of the memory block to hold part of X;
   M - size of memory to hold the nodes of one sub-tree
   output: forest of suffix trees on disk

1 create collection $\mathcal{P}$ of p variable-sized prefixes s.t. ST for each prefix fits in M;
2 **foreach** *prefix Pr in $\mathcal{P}$* **do**
3   generate $Front(Pr)$ array of suffix start positions;
4   set offset for each suffix in $Front(Pr)$ to 0;
5 **end**
6 **foreach** *prefix Pr in $\mathcal{P}$* **do**
7   buildSuffixTreeWavefront($Front(Pr), X, b$);
8 **end**

Wavefront builds a forest of sub-trees. All the suffixes in each subtree ST_i share the same prefix P_i. First, the algorithm collects some statistics about the input string to ensure that the subtree for each prefix can be built entirely in RAM. For this, a collection of variable-length prefixes is created by a procedure similar to the one described for the *Trellis* algorithm in Section 2.4.2. At the end of this operation, for each prefix P_i we have an array of start positions for suffixes that start with P_i.

To illustrate, let us consider a sample input string $X = ababcababd$. At the end of the prefix set building step, we have for prefix $P_1 = a$ an array of suffixes which start with a: $[S_1, S_3, S_6, S_8]$. Subtree ST_1 will contain the leaf nodes for each of these suffixes.

The construction of ST_i is performed independently for each prefix P_i. The memory in *Wavefront* is holding *one block* of size b of the input string and the subtree for a given prefix, and hence the working memory has a constant size. The insertion of suffixes into the tree is performed as in the brute-force algorithm. However, the limitations here are that we can see only b characters of X at each step. Further, we have a partially built suffix tree that does not contain actual characters on its edge-labels, but random positions in the input string. The main idea is to build ST_i by incrementally updating its topology, based only on the available information about b characters and the topology known from the previous iteration. And so, the update of ST_i is performed in *waves*. After each wave, there are unresolved pieces of the tree topology below some nodes, which are stored in a front array (hence the *Wavefront* name of the algorithm). For each wave, the corresponding suffixes are inserted into ST_i, and at each suffix start position we know only its prefix of length b. With each wave, the entire input string is scanned. The edge-labels of the partially built tree, however, contain only actual labels for a current input block B_i.

Let us examine the construction of ST_1 in our example. Suppose that X is very large, and that we cannot hold in main memory more than 3 characters of X at a time. Two waves of the algorithm

---

Function buildSuffixTreeWavefront

    input : array $Front$ for a given prefix; block size b; string X on disk

    output: suffix trees for a given prefix on disk

1 initialize empty tree ST;

2 set node link for each suffix in $Front$ to the *root* node of ST;

3 **for** $i = 1, \cdots, N - b$ **do**

4      $B_i = X[i \cdots i + b]$ - load mappings from positions i to $i + b$ to actual characters of X into RAM;

5   **foreach** *suffix S_j in $Front$* **do**

6   read *start Position*, *offset*, and link node v of S_j from $Front$;

7   match characters of X starting from $j + offset$ to edge labels of ST below v;

8   **while** *the matching characters in ST are known from B_i* **do**

9   advance *offset*;

10   **end**

11   **if** *there is a mismatch with a character which is known from B_i next to node u* **then**

12   **if** *u is implicit* **then**

13   make it explicit internal node;

14   **end**

15   add child to u with the leaf node for S_j;

16   remove S_j from $Front$ array;

17   **end**

18   **if** *the next character of X cannot be compared to character of ST (not in B_i)* **then**

19   **if** *u is implicit* **then**

20   make it explicit internal node;

21   **end**

22   link S_j in $Front$ array to u;

23   **end**

24   **end**

25 **end**

---

are presented in Figures 3.1 and 3.2. Each figure represents one wave in the construction of the suffix tree for all the suffixes of string $X = ababcababd$ that start with prefix a. In the first wave, only characters at positions from 1 to 3 are known for the edge-labels of the tree. We insert each suffix in order by scanning each suffix in $[S_1, S_3, S_6, S_8]$ at most $b = 3$ characters in each iteration. We build the suffix tree based on our knowledge of the first 3 characters on its edge-labels. For example, for suffix S_2 the complete topology is found already after the first iteration, since this suffix differs from S_1 already in its third character. For suffix S_6 we do not know the character at position 4 of the edge-label, and thus we cannot resolve the topology of the tree for this suffix. The temporary internal

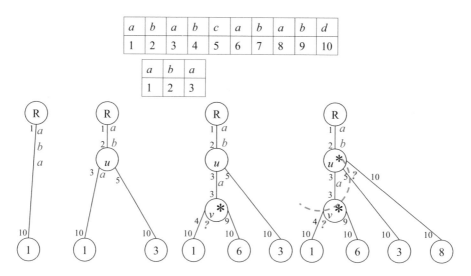

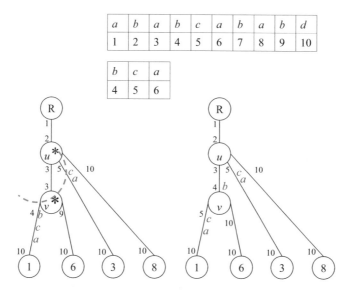

Figure 3.1: The first wave of the *Wavefront* algorithm. Only the 3 first characters of *X* are accessible. The topology of the edges labeled by the positions of these first 3 characters are resolved. The dotted line represents the wavefront array. In the next wave, only unresolved nodes in the wavefront array are observed and resolved.

Figure 3.2: The second wave of the *Wavefront* algorithm. The second block of the input string is in main memory. The corresponding edges and nodes are updated.

node $v*$ is created. This node is added to the front array, and the topology below it is resolved in the next wave. Once the second block of the input string is in memory and we compare unresolved edge labels, this node will be converted into a complete node v, as shown in Figure 3.2.

The topology of the tree is resolved from top to bottom, with the wavefront array of implicit nodes moving down the tree. The topology part closer to the root node is resolved first. This method of top-down construction is possible due to the following observation: the positions that label an edge-label of any suffix tree node are always greater than the positions on the edge-label of its parent. This holds for the brute–force suffix insertion, which was used in this algorithm, i.e., when each current suffix S_j starts to the right of any previously added suffix S_i ($j > i$).

This fact is demonstrated in Figure 3.3. When we add to the tree a new suffix S_j, the incoming edge of the leaf for suffix S_i is split to create a new internal node u and a new leaf for S_j; u is now a parent of two children: the previous leaf for suffix S_i and the new leaf node for S_j. The positions on the incoming edge of a leaf node for S_i are greater than the positions on the incoming edge of node u since both these labels represent two consecutive parts of the same suffix S_i. Since the next suffix S_j starts after S_i ($j > i$ by construction) and since it shares the $i_1 - i + 1$ first characters with suffix S_i, the positions on the edge to the new leaf j are greater than those on the edge leading to leaf i. Thus, they are also greater than the positions on the incoming edge of u – its parent node.

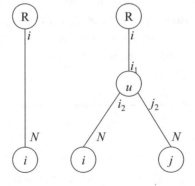

Figure 3.3: The main observation of the *Wavefront* algorithm: $j_2 > i_1$.

Using this top-down approach, *Wavefront* never loads the oversized input string into main memory, and all the multiple scans of the input string are performed sequentially. For each prefix P_i it performs N/b waves, and each wave performs scanning of the entire input string of size N. There are in total pN/b scans of the input of size N, where p, the total number of different prefixes, roughly corresponds to the *input-to-memory ratio* $r = N/M$: $p = CN/M$. Here, C is a constant that represents the double size of each suffix tree node, and is in practice about 50. There are, therefore, $50N^2/MB$ sequential scans. In each scan at most b characters are scanned starting from N/p positions. The running time of *Wavefront* on a single machine is therefore $O(N^3 b/Mb) = O(50r N^2)$. The construction can be performed in parallel for each sub-tree, and this parallel construction does not require machines with large RAM, since the algorithm works in a small constant-size working space.

3.2   THE B^2ST ALGORITHM

Another approach is to extend the multi-way merge sort construction algorithm of Section 2.4.3 to the case of inputs that are larger than the main memory. Let r be the input-to-memory ratio $r = N/M$, where M is the size in bytes of the available RAM, and let $r > 1$. Recall that in order to use the external memory two-phase multi-way merge-sort, we partition X into (slightly overlapping) partitions and lexicographically sort the suffixes in each partition. We can do this in main memory by using any of the best algorithms for in-memory suffix sorting. Then, we output to disk the suffix arrays for suffixes in different partitions.

A problem arises when we want to merge these suffix arrays. In the simple case of merging sorted lists of keys, the relative order of elements from any two different lists is determined by comparing these elements. However, in our case, all we have are the starting positions of suffixes from different partitions, since this is all the information we can store in suffix arrays. This does not help in determining the relative lexicographical order of suffixes from different partitions, because our sorting keys are the substrings of X (not their starting positions).

A naïve approach would compare two suffixes from different partitions by performing random accesses to X, which in this case is on disk. This would lead to $O(N)$ *random* disk I/Os, a prohibitive amount even for small N. Be reminded that the size N of our input string is several times larger than the available main memory ($r > 1$).

Algorithm 8: The B^2ST algorithm.

    input : string X of length N on disk; memory M to hold part of X
    output: forest of suffix trees of X on disk, divided by lexicographic intervals

1 partition X into k substrings $X_1, \cdots, X_k$ such that concatenation of each pair $X_i X_j$
    ($i < j$) fits in M;
2 **for** $i = 1, \cdots, k - 1$ **do**
3   **for** $j = i + 1, \cdots, k$ **do**
4   concatenate $X_i X_j$;
5   build suffix array with *lcp* $SA(X_i X_j)$;
6   write $SA(X_i)$ into a separate file on disk;
7   write order array $R_{i,j}$ with *lcp* into a separate file on disk;
8   **end**
9 **end**
10 mergePartitionsBBST()

Function mergePartitionsBBST

    input : k suffix arrays $SA(X_j)$ for sub-strings of X on disk;
    $k(k-1)/2$ order arrays $R_{i,j}$ on disk;
    output: forest of suffix trees of X on disk, divided by lexicographic intervals

1 allocate k suffix array input buffers $IB(SA)$; $k(k-1)/2$ order array input buffers $IB(R)$ and 1 output buffer OB;

2 initialize suffix tree ST in OB;

3 **for** $i = 1, \cdots, k-1$ **do**

4   read part of $SA(X_i)$ from disk into buffer $IB(SA_i)$;

5   **for** $j = i+1, \cdots, k$ **do**

6   read part of $R_{i,j}$ into $IB(R_{i,j})$

7   **end**

8 **end**

9 create *heap* of size k;

10 insert first element of each $IB(SA)$ into *heap*;

11 to compare elements of $IB(SA_i)$ and $IB(SA_j)$ consult the comparison bit in $IB(R_{i,j})$;

12 **while** *heap is not empty* **do**

13   pop the smallest suffix S_x of partition X_p from the top of *heap*;

14   read *lcp* of this suffix with the last inserted suffix from the corresponding $IB(R)$;

15   add to ST an internal node at depth *lcp* and a leaf node for suffix S_x;

16   **if** *OB is full* **then**

17   write ST to disk;

18   initialize new ST in OB;

19   **end**

20   **if** $IB(SA_p)$ *is empty and not the end of* $SA(X_p)$ **then**

21   fill $IB(SA_p)$ with the next suffixes;

22   **end**

23   when needed refill any order buffer containing p: $IB(R_{p,*})$ or $IB(R_{*,p})$;

24   **if** $IB(SA_p)$ *is not empty* **then**

25   insert next suffix S_y of partition X_p into *heap*;

26   to rebalance heap consult the comparison bit in the corresponding order array;

27   **end**

28 **end**

Algorithm B^2ST[1] solves the problem of ordering suffixes from different partitions by avoiding actual character comparisons. Instead, it deduces the necessary information about the relative order

---

[1] B^2ST stands for Big string Big tree Suffix Tree.

and the lcp of any two suffixes from special structures – *pairwise order arrays* – which are created in advance, in the first phase of the merge-sort. In the merge phase the order arrays are uploaded sequentially from their disk runs. Thus, there is no need to access the entire input string in the merge phase, and we completely avoid random I/Os to the disk-based input string. The pseudocode is given in Algorithm 8.

The first step of the B^2ST algorithm is partitioning the input string X of size N into k partitions such that $k = 2r$ (recall that $r = N/M$ is the input to memory ratio). We require that memory M accommodates the concatenation of any pair of partitions. An example in Figure 3.4 shows the partitioning of $X = abababaaabbabbbabaabab$. The memory designated for the input string can accommodate only 2 partitions of size no more than 8 bytes each.

Partition A					Partition B					Partition C					Partition D				
a	b	a	b	a	a	a	b	b	a	b	b	b	a	b	a	a	b	a	b
1	2	3	4	5	1	2	3	4	5	1	2	3	4	5	1	2	3	4	5

Figure 3.4: Partitioning of input string $X = abababaaabbabbbabaabab$ into four partitions. The combined size of each partition pair with their tails must be less than the size of main memory M.

In the next step we generate a suffix array with lcp for each pair of partitions. We concatenate every possible pair u, v of partitions ($0 \leq u < k - 1, u + 1 \leq v < k, u < v$) into string X_uX_v. We load this input into the main memory and build suffix array SA_{uv} with corresponding lcp values for each suffix. We can use any algorithm from Section 2.4 that can build a suffix array with lcp information using disk space for any input, given that this input fits entirely into main memory. The example in Figure 3.5 shows how the suffix array with LCP looks like for the pair of partitions A, B.

From each SA_{uv} ($u < v$), we extract two structures: (1) the suffix array SA_u for partition X_u and (2) an "order array" R_{uv} of size $|X_u| + |X_v|$. The *order array* R_{uv} contains the lcp entries of SA_{uv} plus the partition ID information. Since each R_{uv} contains information about two partitions only, we just need to use *one bit* to represent the partition ID in R_{uv}. Specifically, we use 0 for u and 1 for v ($u < v$). Figure 3.6 shows SA_A and R_{AB} extracted from SA_{AB} in Figure 3.5. At the end of this step we have on disk k suffix arrays for k partitions (of total size of $O(N)$), plus $k(k - 1)/2$ order arrays for each possible pair of partitions (of total size kN).

This is all the information we need to efficiently perform the next step – the merge. As a result of this merge we produce the suffix tree (or the suffix array with lcp) for the entire input string X. We do this without loading the entire input string into main memory. In fact, we never access X anymore.

In order to merge the suffix arrays of different partitions, we use the information from the order arrays. Notably, all these arrays are accessed sequentially. More specifically, the merge works as follows. As in the classical multi-way merge sort, we have k input buffers for each of the k disk-

Partition A					Partition B									
a	b	a	b	a	a	a	b	b	a	b	b	b		
1	2	3	4	5	1	2	3	4	5	1	2	3		

SA_{AB} (suffix array)										
suffix start	5	1	3	1	2	5	4	2	4	3
	a	a	a	a	a	a	b	b	b	b
	a	a	b	b	b	b	a	a	a	b
	a	b	a	a	b	b	a	b	b	a
	b	b	a	b	a	b	a	a	b	b
	...	...	...	...	...		...	...	...	...
LCP	0	2	1	3	2	3	0	2	3	1
partition bit	A	B	A	A	B	B	A	A	B	B

Figure 3.5: Suffix array with LCP for pair of partitions A and B for the input in Figure 3.4. The total length of both partitions is less than the size of main memory: $|X_A| + |X_B| < M$.

R_{AB}										
LCP	0	2	1	3	2	3	0	2	3	1
partition bit	A	B	A	A	B	B	A	A	B	B

SA_A				
5	3	1	4	2

written to disk

Figure 3.6: Example of an output after pairwise partition sorting. Two structures are extracted from suffix array SA_{AB}: (1) the suffix array of partition A and (2) the order array R_{AB} storing the relative order of suffixes in A and B. These two structures are written to disk.

based suffix arrays. We denote the buffer for a suffix array SA_u by SA_BUF_u. In addition, we use $k(k-1)/2$ input buffers for order arrays. We denote the buffer for an order array R_{uv} by R_BUF_{uv}. Finally, we have an output buffer, ST_BUF, where we collect the nodes of the merged suffix tree before emptying it to disk. The total size of all the buffers is constant and matches the size of the available main memory. The merge proceeds as usual by comparing the top elements of each suffix array buffer, inserting them into a heap, and removing the lexicographically smallest element of the heap to add it to the output suffix tree. In order to compare two entries of, say, SA_BUF_u and SA_BUF_v ($u < v$), while inserting to and rebalancing the heap we consult the partition bit in buffer R_BUF_{uv} under the current pointer. If the bit is 0, we conclude that the current suffix of partition u is lexicographically smaller than the current suffix of partition v, and vice versa. We continue in a similar way until all suffixes are merged. Note, that the disk-resident suffix arrays and the order arrays are read sequentially. This would not be the case if we were consulting the input string X to resolve a relative order for arbitrary suffix start positions of different partitions.

To summarize, during the merge we determine the relative order and the lcp between suffixes from different partitions from the information collected in the pairwise suffix sorting step. The advantage of this is that the information in the order arrays can be accessed sequentially and thus can be kept on disk. Otherwise, we would need to compare substrings of X starting at arbitrary positions.

B^2ST does not require numerous scannings as in *Wavefront*. However, it requires a large temporary disk space. Specifically, we need $D = k^2 p = kN$ bytes of disk space to store the order arrays for all partition pairs. Since the number of partitions is $k = N/M$, from $D = N^2/M$ we can determine the size of the largest input that we can process with M bytes of internal memory and D bytes of disk space. If we substitute the average values for modern computers, $D = 10^{12}$ (1 TB), and $M = 4 \times 10^9$ (4 GB), then we can build suffix trees using such a machine for up to 60 GB of input. Note, however, that disk space is much less expensive than main memory nowadays.

Regarding the execution time, it is clear that the construction of suffix arrays for a pair of partitions can be done in parallel, since each such sorting is independent of the others. The scanning of $O(kN)$ intermediate disk structures in the merge step is very efficient due to the sequential reading.

Because the suffix array construction and LCP computation can be done in linear time, and because we have $k(k-1)/2$ different pair combinations, the running time of the sorting step is $O(kN)$ (where $k = 2r$). In other words, the time is proportional to the total input size and the input-to-memory ratio r (i.e. how many times our input exceeds the available main memory). The suffix arrays and the order arrays produced in this step require $O(kN)$ temporary disk space. In the merge step, the suffix tree of size $O(N)$ is constructed in time linear in N. This requires, however, a complete scan of the intermediate order arrays of size $O(kN)$. Thus, the total running time of the B^2ST algorithm is $O(kN)$.

For comparison, the running time of the *Wavefront* algorithm is $O(kN^2)$.

3.3   SUMMARY

In this chapter, we presented two efficient external-memory suffix tree construction algorithms for very large inputs. Both algorithms are designed to store all inputs, outputs and intermediate data structures on disk, and to access the disk-based data structures sequentially. The *Wavefront* algorithm achieves this by numerous sequential scannings of the input string, while the B^2ST algorithm uses large temporary disk space. These are the first practical algorithms that allow overcoming the input string bottleneck for a fully-scalable construction of suffix trees. Whether the computation can be done more efficiently from the running time or disk space point of view remains an open question.

3.4   BIBLIOGRAPHIC NOTES

The *Wavefront* algorithm was proposed by Ghoting and Makarychev [2009]. B^2ST was introduced by Barsky et al. [2009] and extended by Barsky et al. [2011].

CHAPTER 4

Queries for Disk-based Indexes

In this chapter, we explore how to use the disk-based indexes constructed by the algorithms in chapters 2 and 3 for different queries. In order for the queries to be efficient, we need to organize the indexes on disk in a way that minimizes the number of random disk I/Os when answering queries. We start, in Section 4.1, by discussing different variants of such layouts. In Section 4.2, we present different types of pattern matching using suffix trees. Section 4.3 is devoted to algorithms that use suffix trees for finding repeating and unique substrings.

4.1 INDEX LAYOUTS

First, we need to take into account that on-disk full-text indexes are often too big to be loaded entirely into RAM. Therefore, measures should be taken to optimize their layouts on disk for sequential reads.

We recall that most of the algorithms presented in the previous chapters do not deliver a single suffix tree on disk, but rather a decomposition forest of suffix trees. So far, we discussed that such an organization is useful during the construction. It turns out that this is also necessary for performing efficient queries. If a single suffix tree is of a size that is much larger than the available main memory, then searching for a query pattern Q of length q may incur q random I/Os, plus one random I/O for each occurrence, summing up to $O(q + occ)$ random disk I/Os. The need to decompose the tree into meaningful smaller trees is even more prominent for algorithms that require a depth-first traversal (DFT) of the entire tree. In such cases, the number of random I/Os will be $O(N)$, and the performance of DFT-based algorithms will severely degrade.

Thus, an important practical requirement for the output suffix trees is that each tree can be loaded with one random disk I/O and traversed entirely in main memory. Furthermore, each such tree must have some unique identifier to be located quickly.

These requirements gave raise to several tree partitioning schemes.

4.1.1 PARTITIONING BY PREFIX

Partitioning by prefix is the most commonly used decomposition. For each prefix, there is a separate tree which contains all suffixes sharing this prefix. In order to search for a pattern Q, we need to locate and sequentially load a tree ST_i corresponding to a prefix of Q. Then we find all the occurrences of Q in ST_i. Due to partitioning by prefix, there are no other occurrences of Q to be found in another tree.

For DFS, we sequentially load each tree, and thus the maximum number of random I/Os equals the total number p of such trees.

If the size of each prefix is constant, say P, then the total number of prefixes is $|\Sigma|^P$. Constant-size prefixes are used in Hunt's algorithm (Section 2.2), in distributed and paged suffix trees (Section 2.3.2), and in the *TDD* algorithm (Section 2.4.1). This partitioning scheme works well in practice, except when the (real-life) input data are so skewed that for some prefixes the trees are very small, whereas for others they are so large that they cannot be entirely held in the available main memory.

Variable-length prefixes are used in *Trellis* (Section 2.4.2) and *Wavefront* (Section 3.1) to improve over the data skew problem. This partitioning scheme is described in detail in Section 2.4.2. In order to determine the collection of variable-length prefixes such that all the output trees are of approximately equal size, multiple scans of the input are performed. However, even after that, some trees may be significantly smaller than others.

Partitioning by prefixes has the disadvantage that, for very large inputs, the number of prefixes can be very large. For instance, with equal-length prefixes, the total number of prefixes p grows exponentially with the prefix length. Recall that algorithms such as the one by Hunt, *TDD*, or *Wavefront* perform p iterations over the entire input of size N. A single sequential scan by itself is fast, but the number of scans should not be arbitrarily large. This holds the aforementioned algorithms from scaling up for very large inputs. For example, the authors of *TDD* do not recommend the length of prefixes to be larger than 8 characters, since otherwise the processing time increases dramatically.

4.1.2   PARTITIONING BY INTERVALS

Another way to partition suffix trees is *partitioning by intervals*, used in *DiGeST* (Section 2.4.3) and B^2ST (Section 3.2). If we build the trees from lexicographically sorted suffixes, then we can write the output trees to disk according to lexicographic intervals of the suffixes in each output tree. In order to locate each subtree, the 32-bit prefixes of the lexicographically smallest and the largest suffixes in that tree are recorded in a collection of *dividers*, which divide the resulting forest of trees by their lexicographic intervals. The search starts by locating the proper divider and then loading into memory the entire tree corresponding to this interval. An example is presented in Figure 4.1. All the trees are of equal size. This solves the problem of data skew. In addition, we avoid multiple scans required in order to determine a collection of variable-length prefixes.

Let us now look at a suffix-tree forest produced by *DiGeST* or B^2ST. Such a forest is a collection of suffix trees, each of which is of a small enough size to be quickly loaded into main memory using a sequential disk read. The collection of dividers can be kept entirely in main memory due to the small size of this collection. There is a trade-off between the number of partitions and their size: the number of suffixes in each partition should be adjusted for fast reads. The authors of *DiGeST* have experimentally determined the search-optimal size of each tree to be of $512,000$ nodes per tree, accounting for $256,000$ suffixes. Here, each tree occupies 11.7 MB of disk space. For instance, for an input of 10 GB, the total number of partial trees of this size does not exceed $85,000$, and thus the collection of dividers is kept in main memory during the search.

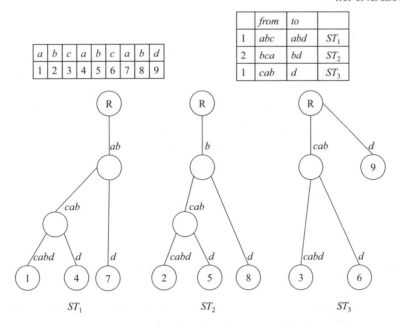

Figure 4.1: Forest of suffix trees for $X = abcabcabd$. The collection of dividers (in the top right corner) is kept in main memory. With each interval we associate a pointer to a corresponding suffix tree. Such a suffix tree can be loaded from disk sequentially.

4.1.3   STRING B-TREE

A *String B-tree* is a combination of B-trees and suffix trees. The String B-tree has the same worst case performance as the B-tree, but handles strings of unbounded length, which are not stored explicitly. Instead, as for suffix trees, the substrings are represented by the corresponding pointers to the input string. Therefore, the input string is not a part of the String B-tree, but is stored independently on disk. Each node of the String B-tree occupies one block and represents a (lexicographically) ordered interval of suffixes, stored in the form of a small suffix tree. An enhanced suffix array can be converted into a String B-tree by grouping corresponding suffixes into corresponding B-tree nodes. The String B-tree can be regarded as an optimized balanced disk layout of a suffix tree.

Note, however, that suffix trees partitioned by intervals (as in *DiGeST* and B^2ST) are also balanced, in the sense that they consist of a forest of equal-sized trees, rather than a single tree with unbalanced topology. Using partitioning by intervals, and keeping the collection of pointing dividers in main memory, we can perform a search with two random disk I/Os only, as compared to $O(\log_b N)$ random accesses for a String B-tree containing N suffixes (for a block size of b). Thus, from a search performance point of view, suffix trees partitioned by prefixes are not less efficient than String B-trees.

Despite the claim that the String B-tree supports updates, these updates have little practicality when dealing with strings of significant length, since for each new string Y we want to index all the $|Y|$ suffixes of this string, thus requiring for each suffix $O(\log_B N)$ random disk I/Os to the String B-tree and $|Y|$ random disk I/Os to the input string (with N being the number of suffixes previously inserted into the String B-tree). Thus, the construction by insertion of a String B-tree for input of size N requires $O(N \log_B N)$ random disk I/Os, which is clearly not practical for large N.

We do not discuss the use of String B-trees in our subsequent discussion. We focus instead on the use of the forest of interval-partitioned suffix trees.

4.2 PATTERN MATCHING WITH DISK-BASED INDEXES

4.2.1 EXACT PATTERN MATCHING

Exact pattern matching (EPM) is to determine at what positions a short query string Q (called *pattern*) occurs as a substring of a larger string X. EPM is often a sub-task in multiple string searching algorithms. The optimal online algorithms for EPM can locate a pattern of length q in a string of length N in time $O(N + q)$, i.e., linear in N. However, for very large strings, which are the focus of this work, this is an unsatisfactory performance.

After the off-line pre-processing of the string into its suffix tree, the pattern can be located in time $O(q + occ)$, where occ is the number of occurrences. However, when the suffix tree resides on disk, we also need to account for the number of random disk I/Os incurred during the search.

We remind the reader that the suffix tree does not store explicitly the labels of its edges. Instead, the edge labels are represented by an ordered pair of integers denoting its start and end positions in the input string.

Let us assume that we have constructed a suffix tree for a string significantly larger than the main memory using either *Wavefront* or B^2ST presented in Chapter 3. In this case, the string resides on disk during the query time. Note that to search for query Q in this tree using a traditional suffix tree traversal of Section 1.4, we (naïvely) compare the characters of Q to the characters of X as indicated by the positions of the edge labels. Such a search, unfortunately, requires multiple random accesses to the input string, and therefore is quite inefficient when X is on disk. In the worst case, this takes q random disk accesses to the input string.

However, random accesses to X during the search can be avoided if we follow the PATRICIA search algorithm, which we call *blind search*. Such a search consists of two phases.

In the first phase, we trace a downward path from the root of the tree to locate a corresponding suffix S_i. We remark that we do not match all the characters of this path to the characters of our query: we start out from the root and only compare some of the characters of Q with the branching characters found in the arcs traversed until we either reach leaf L_i, or no further branching is possible. In the latter case, we choose L_i to be any descending leaf from the last node traversed, say node v.

In the second phase, we read substring $X[i, i + q]$ from the input string X which is on disk, by performing only one random access to the input, instead of q as in the usual suffix tree search.

We compare $X[i, i + q]$ to Q; if both are identical, we report an occurrence of Q in X and collect all the remaining occurrences from the leaf nodes in the subtree of v (if v is not a leaf).

Consider, for example, the suffix tree for $X = ababcababd$ and the two queries $Q_1 = aaab$ and $Q_2 = abab$ shown in Figure 4.2. By matching only the first and the third characters of Q_1 or Q_2, and then verifying the queries against suffix S_1, we perform only one random access to the input string per query. Such an efficient (from the external memory point of view) search does not yet exist for alternative indexing structures, such as suffix arrays.

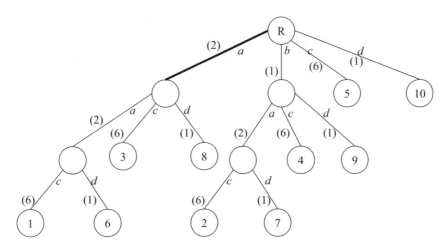

a	b	a	b	c	a	b	a	b	d
1	2	3	4	5	6	7	8	9	10

Figure 4.2: A disk-friendly pattern search in the suffix tree for string $X = ababcababd$. The first characters of each edge are implied by the positions of a child node in the array of children. The length of each edge is shown in brackets, which is deduced from the start and end positions of edge-label substrings. For query $Q_1 = aaab$ we match $Q_1[1]$ and $Q_1[3]$, and then we retrieve the leaf L_1 as well as the substring $X[1, 4]$. Verification fails, since $aaab \neq abab$. Pattern $Q_1 = aaab$ is not a substring of X. For query $Q_2 = abab$ we follow the same path. This time the verification is successful, since $Q_2 = X[1, 4]$. We report all the occurrences of Q_2 in X by collecting leaves 1 and 6. In each case, only one random access to the input string is performed.

In practice, the algorithm performs only 2 random disk I/Os: (1) loading the corresponding suffix tree and (2) reading the substring of X to verify the blind matching. For some patterns that occur multiple times in the input, the search can spread to several trees corresponding to consecutive intervals.

4.2.2   MATCHING ALL SUBSTRINGS OF A QUERY STRING

The problem of *matching all substrings (MAS)* is to determine *all* the occurrences of *each substring* of query Q in a string X.

MAS often arises in bioinformatics as a sub-problem for heuristic local similarity search, such as BLAST, which in the first step finds in the large input string (database) occurrences of *seeds* – short substrings of a long query string. The problem has an efficient solution using an in-memory suffix tree for X. The algorithm for substring matching uses additional edges connecting nodes of the suffix tree, called *suffix links*. Suffix links have been already mentioned in the context of the linear-time suffix tree construction (see Section 2.3). Here we show how to use them for searching substrings of query string Q.

We remind that a *suffix link* is a directed edge from a suffix tree node v that represents the path corresponding to a substring αx to another node u that represents substring x, where α is a single character, and x is an arbitrary substring. Suffix links in the suffix tree for $X = abababc$ are shown in Figure 4.3 as dotted arrows. For the $\star$-node that represents substring $abab$, the suffix link leads to $\star\star$-node that represents substring bab. In turn, the outgoing suffix link from the $\star\star$-node leads to a $\star\star\star$-node - the end of path for substring ab.

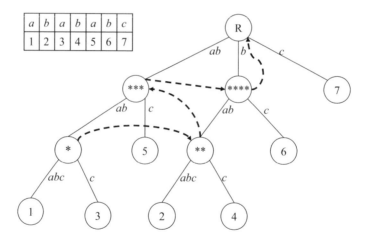

Figure 4.3: Suffix tree with suffix links (dotted arrows) for input string $X = abababc$. The search for all substrings of query string $Q = babac$ is performed by matching suffix $S_1(Q) = babac$ starting from the root, and then the search for the rest of suffixes continues not from the root, but by traversing the suffix tree following the suffix links.

If we want to locate occurrences of all substrings of query string $Q = babac$, the naïve approach is to match each suffix and each prefix of Q to a path from the root of the suffix tree (see Figure 4.3). This would require $O(q^3)$ character comparisons, which can be expensive when the length q of Q is large. By using suffix links the task can be accomplished in time $O(q + occ)$, which is optimal, because q is the size of the input and occ is the size of the output. The process is as follows.

We start by matching characters of suffix $S_1(Q) = babac$ to a path in the suffix tree, successfully matching the first four characters. The occurrences of prefixes of $S_1(Q)$ can be collected from the leaves in the subtrees of the ★★★★-node and ★★-node. Namely,

b occurs at position 6;

bab – at position 4;

$baba$ – at position 2.

Next, instead of matching the next suffix $S_2(Q) = abac$ starting from the root, we follow the suffix link from the ★★-node to the ★★★-node and collect occurrences of prefixes of $S_2(Q)$ from the underlying leaves:

ab – at position 5;

aba – at positions 1 and 3.

Again, from the ★★★-node we jump to the ★★★★-node where we collect occurrences of substring ba, that is 2 and 4.

Finally, from the ★★★★-node we jump to the root and collect occurrences of substrings a and c. Observe that we have compared only q symbols in total.

The suffix links, therefore, represent shortcuts that allow navigating across the suffix tree faster. Moreover, if the path is found for substring αx, then there must be a path for substring x; after all, this is a tree of all suffixes, and x is the suffix of αx. This allows skipping the matching of characters after αx has been matched.

However, for partitioned disk-based suffix trees suffix links are not very useful. If the suffix tree of Figure 4.3 is partitioned into multiple sub-trees and these sub-trees reside on disk and cannot be simultaneously held in main memory, then jumping across such sub-trees following suffix links will be too expensive. The example for the same query $Q = babac$ and $X = ababababc$ in Figure 4.4 demonstrates that. The problem here is that the search is dominated by the number of *random* disk I/Os rather than by character comparisons after a sub-tree is already in RAM.

On the other hand, by grouping suffixes of Q into two sets according to the partitions of this suffix tree and then performing the blind search for each set will lead to a better performance: in this case the sub-tree that has been already searched is not accessed again. Hence, for partitioned on-disk suffix trees the use of the suffix links is limited.

The *Trellis* and *Wavefront* algorithms propose a method of adding suffix links in a post-construction phase, and show that the process is quite expensive. In addition, they do not present an application where the use of suffix links connecting nodes of different sub-trees on disk will lead to an improved query performance.

4.2.3   APPROXIMATE PATTERN MATCHING

The problem of *approximate pattern matching (APM)* is to find all occurrences of query string Q in string X, such that these occurrences are allowed to have up to k errors, that is substitutions, deletions

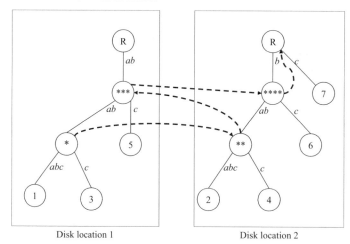

Figure 4.4: Partitioned suffix sub-trees with suffix links between them for the same input string $X = ababab c$ as in Figure 4.3. Here, the shortcut function of the suffix links is not beneficial since for this case it implies jumping from one random disk location to another.

or insertions of a symbol. For example, for $Q = bcc$, $X = abbabc$, and $k = 1$, an approximate occurrence of Q in X is at position 5 of X: the substring $X[5, 6] = bc$ matches bcc with 1 error – deletion of symbol c. APM has important applications in bioinformatics, where very often patterns do not occur in their exact form, but with a small number of errors.

The naïve search for occurrences of Q in X would be to compare each suffix of X with Q using dynamic programming, and once there are more than k errors between some prefix of a suffix of X and Q, abandon this suffix and check the next one. A similar procedure is performed if we use suffix trees for solving APM. The big advantage of the suffix tree is that it groups together all repeating substrings of X, thus only distinct prefixes of suffixes of X are compared with Q (only once). Obviously, this is beneficial for inputs that contain a large number of repeating substrings, which is in general the case for DNA sequences.

APM for $Q = bcc$, $X = abbabc$, and $k = 1$ using a suffix tree is shown in Figure 4.5. If we know that the number of errors between prefix ab of suffixes S_1 and S_4 and bcc is greater than one, we do not need to compare further below the node marked by X, and we can abandon the entire sub-tree below this node. We abandon the rest of the paths after checking prefix bab and prefix bba, and the only solution is pattern bc, which starts at position 5 of X.

APM is a computationally expensive process, and it can be accelerated by the use of suffix trees, but only in the case when X is in main memory so that each character is read without incurring random disk access. Note that for APM, the entire suffix tree needs to be traversed. The blind search employed for EPM does not work here; we need to compare actual characters of X according to the

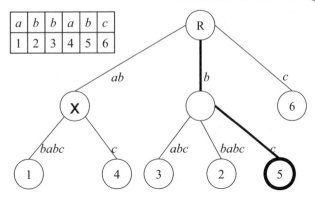

Figure 4.5: Example of the approximate matching of query string $Q = bcc$ and input string $X = abbabc$, using the suffix tree for X.

positions indicated on edge-labels of the suffix tree, and this may incur $O(N)$ random accesses to X. An efficient solution to APM for X that is too big to fit in main memory is an open problem.

4.3   REPEATING AND UNIQUE SUBSTRINGS

In this section, we discuss other types of queries which can be performed using disk-based suffix trees: queries about repetitive and unique substrings. Repetitions are very common in DNA sequences. Families of repeating sequences account for about one third of the Human genome. The repetitions have numerous practical uses. For example, genetic mapping requires the identification of features (or markers) in DNA that are highly variable among individuals. Short repetitive substrings called tandem repeats are just such markers. They vary in number between individuals and are used in the genetic-level search for defective genes, in forensic DNA fingerprinting, and many other applications. The important problem of finding repetitive substrings can be greatly facilitated by suffix trees. The same is true for finding unique substrings, which occur only once in the entire input string.

4.3.1   MAXIMAL REPEATS

A *maximal repeating pair* in input string X is a pair of identical substrings α and β, such that the character to the immediate left (right) of α is different from the character to immediate left (right) of β. That is, extending α or β to either side will break the equality of two substrings. We call each maximal repeating pair a *maximal repeat (MR)*, and each MR can be uniquely identified by a triple: (start position of α, start position of β, and their length). For example, in $X = abcabcabd$, $abcab$ is an MR and its representing triple is $(1, 4, 5)$. The repeating substrings $X[1-5]$ and $X[4-8]$ cannot be extended to the left or to the right.

The problem of finding all MRs in X can be solved in linear time using the suffix tree of X. The suffix tree for $X = abcabcabd$ is presented in Figure 4.6. The intuition behind the algorithm

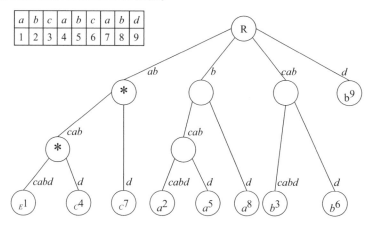

Figure 4.6: Suffix tree for $X = abcabcabd$ with the leaves marked by a symbol to the immediate left of the corresponding suffix start position (ϵ represents an empty string). This information is used in order to check whether the left extension of the repeat is possible. The nodes corresponding to the maximal repeats are marked by $\star$.

for finding MRs is as follows. Because the suffix tree contains all the distinct substrings of X, if the subtree induced by some path branches into several nodes, then the substring labeling this path is a repeating substring, i.e., it occurs as a prefix of more than one suffix. In order to find *maximal* repeats, we only need to consider internal nodes of the suffix tree, since if the path ends in the middle of an edge, then it can be extended up to the next internal node. For example, substring *abca* marks such a path of non-maximal repeating substring. Each internal node of the suffix tree represents a potential maximal repeat since its path-label is already maximal to the right – there are distinct characters labeling the branching edges. This leads to the conclusion that there are at most N MRs in a string X of size N.

However, not every internal node represents a maximal repeat, because it might be the case that the substring represented by a path to this node can be extended to the *left*. In order to check this left character during the traversal of the tree, and to not access the input string, the immediate left characters can be recorded on each leaf node in advance during the tree construction. Then, during the depth-first traversal of the suffix tree, the algorithm marks each internal node as being the root of either a subtree with leaves that have distinct left characters, or a subtree without any leaf offering some distinct character. Substrings corresponding to the latter internal nodes can be extended to the left, thus these internal nodes do not contribute an MR. As an example see Figure 4.6. The algorithm reports only $(1, 4, 5)$ and $(1, 7, 2)$ as MRs. The other internal nodes contain child leaves with identical left characters.

This is the first algorithm based on the depth-first-traversal of the entire tree, which considers only the tree topology.[1] Hence, it is efficient for a disk-based setting considering the partitioned tree layouts. It will perform a sequential read of the entire suffix tree from disk, traverse it in main memory, and collect MRs without knowing the characters of the edge-labels (assuming the left characters on the leaves were added during the tree construction). The MRs can then be reported as triples of positions and length. The extraction of the corresponding actual substrings might, however, incur random I/Os to the input string.

4.3.2   COMMON AND UNIQUE SUBSTRINGS

In the same spirit, we can use suffix trees to find identical substrings in multiple input strings. If we add to the suffix tree more than one input string, then we obtain a modification called a *generalized suffix tree for a set of strings*. The tree contains all suffixes of each input string, and requires an additional identifier of the string id on the edge-labels. An example of the generalized suffix tree for strings $A = abbab$ and $B = babab$ is shown in Figure 4.7.

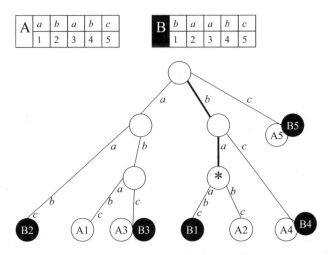

Figure 4.7: The generalized suffix tree for input strings $A = abbab$ and $B = babab$. All substrings common to both A and B can be found in time linear in the total input length. The common substrings end in the nodes that have leaves from both A and B in their corresponding subtrees, such as the node where the path for *ba* (shown in bold) ends.

Using a generalized suffix tree, we can find all substrings common to both input strings. In fact, the common substrings correspond to the labels of any path that induces a subtree with leaves from different strings. For an example, consider the internal node reached by path *ba* highlighted in Figure 4.7.

[1] The APM algorithm in the previous section required the information about the actual characters of the input string.

This efficient solution to the common substrings problem may have an interesting application for sequences of different genomes: in terms of genomic information, the sufficiently long substrings occurring in multiple genomes of different species point to conserved regions, which were preserved during the evolution. The possibility of efficiently finding these important common regions is greatly facilitated by the use of suffix trees.

The same is true for unique substrings. The example in Figure 4.8 shows how to find substrings unique to a given input string. These are substrings that label a path that does not induce a sub-tree with leaves from distinct input strings.

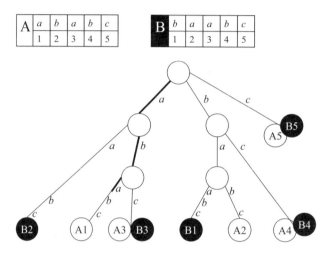

Figure 4.8: The substring *aba*, unique to input string $A = abbab$, is shown as a bold path in this generalized suffix tree for $A = abbab$ and $B = babab$. Any substring that ends on a leaf edge is unique, since it occurs only once; otherwise, it would label a path to some internal node.

Finding common substrings is another example of the depth-first traversal of suffix trees, which is very efficient also in disk-based settings: the algorithm reads small partial trees sequentially and does not require referencing to the input strings, taking into account only tree topology.

4.4   SUMMARY

In this chapter we presented several basic queries which use full-text indexes. We discussed which of them can be as efficient on disk as in-memory. Among the considered queries, we showed that exact pattern matching, computing repetitions, and finding common substrings can be well served (incurring only a small number of random I/Os) by disk-based suffix trees. On the other hand, the problems of all substring matching and approximate pattern matching require new non-trivial solutions for the case when both the suffix tree and the input string are on disk.

4.5   BIBLIOGRAPHIC NOTES

The algorithms performing exact pattern matching without preprocessing input string X, and in time linear in the size of X, are from Knuth et al. [1977] and Boyer and Moore [1977]. PATRICIA search (blind search in our notation) was originally described by Morrison [1968]. String B-trees were introduced by Ferragina and Grossi [1999]. The algorithm for approximate pattern matching is from Navarro and Baeza-Yates [2000]. The rest of algorithms are adopted from Gusfield [1997].

CHAPTER 5

Conclusions and Open Problems

In this book we presented practical algorithms for disk-based construction and querying of full-text indexes. The algorithms perform well in practice and can be successfully used for indexing all substrings in databases of long strings, especially of sequenced genomes. We believe that these algorithms are important steps towards a fully scalable solution for constructing full-text indexes on disk for inputs of any type and size. Once this is done, a whole world of new possibilities will be opened, especially in the field of biological sequence analysis.

In order to use disk-based full-text indexes to their full potential, there are some problems that need to be addressed in future research. Specifically, we identify (a) improving the efficiency of disk-based suffix tree construction and (b) scaling-up the use of these suffix trees for complex tasks (such as approximate pattern matching) to be the most important open problems. We elaborate more on these problems in the following.

5.1 NEED FOR BETTER CONSTRUCTION ALGORITHMS

As we know from Section 2.1, all full-text indexes – excluding the plain suffix array – can be converted into each other by a disk-friendly sequential scan. This means that it is sufficient to develop the most basic form of the full-text index: the suffix array with the lcp.

There are promising theoretical results for constructing the plain suffix array, which can be adopted for sequential memory access. An example is the Difference Cover algorithm by Kärkkäinen et al. [2006]. However, the suffix array needs to be augmented with the lcp information in order to be converted into any other full-text index. Though there exist linear-time, space-efficient, and easy-to-implement lcp computation algorithms (see for example Kasai et al. [2001], Manzini [2004]), these algorithms perform random access to at least one intermediate array of size N. Thus, these algorithms would severely degrade in performance once N is larger than the main memory. This limits the scalability of indexing to only strings which can be held entirely in RAM. Theoretical results for computing the lcp array in external memory settings were reported by Chiang et al. [1995]. These results are based on range minima queries, performed using special tree-like data structures and an external memory sort of queries to minimize random disk I/Os. However, so far, no one has been able to efficiently implement these ideas.

Note also that the best practical algorithms presented in Section 2.4 and Chapter 3, optimized for sequential disk access, have an internal running time that is asymptotically quadratic in N. Although on average this time is only $O(N \log N)$, it increases dramatically if we construct a generalized suffix tree for very similar DNA sequences. For example, in order to compare DNA sequences of different genomes of the same species (c.f. "the 1000 genomes project", Karow [2008]), when building a generalized suffix tree for these sequences, all the algorithms presented in this book will perform poorly. The only algorithm not suffering from this problem is B^2ST (Section 3.2). However, it performs in time $O(rN)$, where $r = N/M$ is the input-to-memory ratio. Due to this fact, it is better to perform the pairwise sorting step of this algorithm in parallel on multiple machines, in order for the construction to scale to the size of the entire Genbank (more than 100 GB of input).

5.2   NEED FOR BETTER QUERY ALGORITHMS

With a look at the potential applications of the on-disk full-text indexes in Chapter 4, we notice scalability limitations of some of the presented algorithms. If we perform the task of approximate pattern matching of query string Q in text X, we need to compare actual characters of the string with actual characters corresponding to the edge-labels of the suffix tree. This incurs massive random I/Os to input string X. Therefore, the use of suffix trees for this task is limited to inputs that fit in main memory. A fully-scalable, efficient, APM is an open problem.

The range minima queries used for the computation of the *lcp* information can also be used for finding the lowest common ancestor node of two suffixes in the suffix tree. The algorithms based on constant-time retrieval of the lowest common ancestor include an algorithm for APM by Landau and Vishkin [1986] and an algorithm for finding common substrings for a set of multiple strings in time $O(N)$ described by Gusfield [1997]. These algorithms are not very efficient for disk-based indexes because no practical implementation of the range-minima queries for a disk setting exists. Recent advances in the adaptation of the lowest common ancestor retrieval to the disk access computational model are presented by Demaine et al. [2009]. These are interesting theoretical results, whose implementation will require in practice multiple calls to a sub-routine of the external-memory sort, and this can make the practical efficiency of these methods quite questionable. All the lowest common ancestor algorithms proposed for disk are quite involved and challenging to implement. Thus, this would be an interesting area for an ambitious researcher.

A last note is about the usefulness of suffix links for algorithms on disk-based suffix trees. Recall that suffix links connect each internal node representing some substring αx (where α is one character long) of X with some other internal node where the path for substring x ends. The suffix links – a by-product of the main memory linear time construction algorithms – can be useful by themselves as demonstrated in Section 4.2.2 using the example of finding occurrences for all substrings of the query Q in string X. Suffix links can be recovered in a post-processing step of the disk-based suffix tree construction. We believe that these recovered suffix links in the external memory settings are of a limited use, since a link can lead to a different subtree laid out in a distant disk locations. This means that the assumed "constant-time" jump following a suffix link can cause, in fact, an entire random disk I/O. Hence, the algorithms whose efficiency relies on the use of suffix links (such as the algorithms of Kurtz and Schleiermacher [1999], Kurtz et al. [2004]), might require new, non-trivial, adaptations when moved from in-memory to on-disk settings.

Bibliography

A. Apostolico and W. Szpankowski. Self-alignments in words and their applications. *J. Algorithms*, 13(3):446–467, 1992. DOI: 10.1016/0196-6774(92)90049-I Cited on page(s) 39

M. Barsky, U. Stege, A. Thomo, and C. Upton. A new method for indexing genomes using on-disk suffix trees. In *Proc. Int. Conf. on Information and Knowledge Management*, pages 649–658, 2008. DOI: 10.1145/1458082.1458170 Cited on page(s) 41

M. Barsky, U. Stege, A. Thomo, and C. Upton. Suffix trees for very large genomic sequences. In *Proc. Int. Conf. on Information and Knowledge Management*, pages 1417–1420, 2009. DOI: 10.1145/1645953.1646134 Cited on page(s) 53

M. Barsky, U. Stege, and A. Thomo. Suffix trees for inputs larger than main memory. *Inf. Syst.*, 36 (3):644–654, 2011. DOI: 10.1016/j.is.2010.11.001 Cited on page(s) 53

S.J. Bedathur and J.R. Haritsa. Engineering a fast online persistent suffix tree construction. In *Proc. 20th Int. Conf. on Data Engineering*, 2004. DOI: 10.1109/ICDE.2004.1320040 Cited on page(s) 40

R. Boyer and J. Moore. A fast string searching algorithm. *Commun. ACM*, 20(10):762–772, 1977. DOI: 10.1145/359842.359859 Cited on page(s) 67

Y. Chiang, M. Goodrich, E. Grove, R. Tamassia, D. Vengroff, and J. Vitter. External-memory graph algorithms. In *Proc. 6th Annual ACM-SIAM Symp. on Discrete Algorithms*, 1995. Cited on page(s) 69

R. Clifford and M.J. Sergot. Distributed and paged suffix trees for large genetic databases. In *Proc. 14th Annual Symp. on Combinatorial Pattern Matching*, pages 70–82, 2003. DOI: 10.1007/3-540-44888-8_6 Cited on page(s) 40

R. de la Briandais. File searching using variable length keys. In *Proc. IRE-AIEE-ACM western joint computer conference*, pages 295–298, 1959. DOI: 10.1145/1457838.1457895 Cited on page(s) 15

E. Demaine, G. Landau, and O. Weimann. On cartesian trees and range minimum queries. In *36th Int. Colloquium on Automata, Languages, and Programming*, pages 341–353, 2009. DOI: 10.1007/978-3-642-02927-1_29 Cited on page(s) 70

P. Ferragina and R. Grossi. The string B-tree: a new data structure for string search in external memory and its applications. *J. of the ACM*, 46(2):236–280, 1999. DOI: 10.1145/301970.301973 Cited on page(s) 67

J. Fischer, V. Mäkinen, and G. Navarro. An(other) entropy-bounded compressed suffix tree. In *Proc. 19th Annual Symp. on Combinatorial Pattern Matching*, pages 152–165, 2008a. DOI: 10.1007/978-3-540-69068-9_16 Cited on page(s) 15

J. Fischer, V. Mäkinen, and N. Välimäki. Space efficient string mining under frequency constraints. In *Proc. 2008 IEEE Int. Conf. on Data Mining*, pages 193–202, 2008b. DOI: 10.1109/ICDM.2008.32 Cited on page(s) 15

E. Fredkin. Trie memory. *Commun. ACM*, 3(9):490–499, 1960. DOI: 10.1145/367390.367400 Cited on page(s) 15

A. Ghoting and K. Makarychev. Serial and parallel methods for I/O efficient suffix tree construction. In *Proc. ACM SIGMOD Int. Conf. on Management of Data*, pages 827–840, 2009. DOI: 10.1145/1559845.1559931 Cited on page(s) 53

R. Giegerich and S. Kurtz. From ukkonen to mccreight and weiner: A unifying view of linear-time suffix tree construction. *Algorithmica*, 19(3):331–353, 1997. DOI: 10.1007/PL00009177 Cited on page(s) 40

R. Giegerich, S. Kurtz, and J. Stoye. Efficient implementation of lazy suffix trees. *Software—Practice and Experience*, 33(11):1035–1049, 2003. DOI: 10.1002/spe.535 Cited on page(s) 15, 41

D. Gusfield. *Algorithms on Strings, Trees, and Sequences: Computer Science and Computational Biology.* Cambridge University Press, 1997. Cited on page(s) 8, 15, 67, 70

E. Hunt, M.P. Atkinson, and R.W. Irving. A database index to large biological sequences. *VLDB J.*, 7(3):139–148, 2001. Cited on page(s) 39

A. Jacobs. The pathologies of big data. *Commun. ACM*, 52(8):36–44, 2009. DOI: 10.1145/1536616.1536632 Cited on page(s) 14

J. Kärkkäinen, P. Sanders, and S. Burkhardt. Linear work suffix array construction. *J. ACM*, 53(6): 918–936, 2006. DOI: 10.1145/1217856.1217858 Cited on page(s) 69

J. Karow. Group unveils "1,000 genomes" study to map genetic variants using new sequencing tools. http://www.genomeweb.com/sequencing/, 2008. Cited on page(s) 70

T. Kasai, G. Lee, H. Arimura, S. Arikawa, and K. Park. Linear-time longest-common-prefix computation in suffix arrays and its applications. In *Proc. 12th Annual Symp. on Combinatorial Pattern Matching*, pages 181–192, 2001. DOI: 10.1007/3-540-48194-X_17 Cited on page(s) 69

D. Knuth, J. Morris Jr, and V. Pratt. Fast pattern matching in strings. *SIAM J. on Comput.*, 6(2): 323–350, 1977. DOI: 10.1137/0206024 Cited on page(s) 67

S. Kurtz and C. Schleiermacher. Reputer: fast computation of maximal repeats in complete genomes. *Bioinformatics*, 15(R12):426–427, 1999. DOI: 10.1093/bioinformatics/15.5.426 Cited on page(s) 70

S. Kurtz, A. Phillippy, A.L. Delcher, M. Smoot, M. Shumway, C. Antonescu, and S.L. Salzberg. Versatile and open software for comparing large genomes. *Genome Biology*, 5:R12, 2004. DOI: 10.1186/gb-2004-5-2-r12 Cited on page(s) 70

G. Landau and U. Vishkin. Introducing efficient parallelism into approximate string matching and a new serial algorithm. In *Proc. 18th Annual ACM Symp. on Theory of Computing*, pages 220–230, 1986. DOI: 10.1145/12130.12152 Cited on page(s) 70

U. Manber and E. Myers. Suffix arrays: A new method for on-line string searches. *SIAM J. on Comput.*, 22(5):935–948, 1993. DOI: 10.1137/0222058 Cited on page(s) 15

G. Manzini. Two space saving tricks for linear time lcp array computation. In *Proc. Scandinavian. Workshop on Algorithm Theory*, pages 372–3837, 2004. DOI: 10.1007/978-3-540-27810-8_32 Cited on page(s) 69

E. M. McCreight. A space-economical suffix tree construction algorithm. *J. ACM*, 23(2):262–272, 1976. DOI: 10.1145/321941.321946 Cited on page(s) 15, 40

U. Meyer, P. Sanders, and J. F. Sibeyn, editors. *Algorithms for Memory Hierarchies, Advanced Lectures [Dagstuhl Research Seminar, March 10-14, 2002]*, volume 2625 of *Lecture Notes in Computer Science*. Springer, 2003. Cited on page(s) 39

D. Morrison. Patricia – practical algorithm to retrieve information coded in alphanumeric. *J. ACM*, 15(4):514–534, 1968. DOI: 10.1145/321479.321481 Cited on page(s) 15, 67

G. Navarro and R. Baeza-Yates. A hybrid indexing method for approximate string matching. *J. of Discrete Algorithms*, 1(1):205–209, 2000. Cited on page(s) 40, 67

B. Phoophakdee and M.J. Zaki. Genome-scale disk-based suffix tree indexing. In *Proc. ACM SIGMOD Int. Conf. on Management of Data*, 2007. DOI: 10.1145/1247480.1247572 Cited on page(s) 41

L. Russo, G. Navarro, and A. Oliveira. Dynamic fully-compressed suffix trees. In *Proc. 19th Annual Symp. on Combinatorial Pattern Matching, LNCS 5029*, pages 191–203, 2008. DOI: 10.1007/978-3-540-69068-9_19 Cited on page(s) 15

K. Sadakane. Compressed suffix trees with full functionality. *Theory Comput. Syst.*, 41(4):589–607, 2007. DOI: 10.1007/s00224-006-1198-x Cited on page(s) 15

Y. Tian, S. Tata, R. Hankins, and J. Patel. Practical methods for constructing suffix trees. *The VLDB J.*, 450:219–232, 2007. DOI: 10.1007/s00778-005-0154-8 Cited on page(s) 41

E. Ukkonen. On-line construction of suffix trees. *Algorithmica*, 14(3):249–260, 1995. DOI: 10.1007/BF01206331 Cited on page(s) 40

J. Vitter and M. Shriver. Algorithms for parallel memory: Two-level memories. *Algorithmica*, 12: 110–147, 1994. DOI: 10.1007/BF01185207 Cited on page(s) 15

P. Weiner. Linear pattern matching algorithm. In *IEEE Symp. on Switching and Automata Theory*, pages 1–11, 1973. DOI: 10.1109/SWAT.1973.13 Cited on page(s) 15, 40

Authors' Biographies

MARINA BARSKY

Marina Barsky is a Post-Doctoral Fellow in the Department of Computer Science at the University of Illinois at Urbana-Champaign, US. She received her PhD in Computer Science from the University of Victoria, British Columbia, Canada in 2010. Her PhD research was dedicated to better construction of full-text indexes using disk. Currently she expands her expertise in database management to the field of data mining.

ULRIKE STEGE

Ulrike Stege is an Associate Professor in the Department of Computer Science at the University of Victoria, British Columbia, Canada. She received her PhD in Computer Science from the ETH Zürich – a Science and Technology University in Zürich, Switzerland, in year 2000. Her main research interests are interdisciplinary, including the areas of Parameterized Complexity, Computational Biology, Cognitive Science and Human Problem Solving, and Computer Science Education.

ALEX THOMO

Alex Thomo is an Associate Professor in the Department of Computer Science at the University of Victoria, British Columbia, Canada. He received his PhD in Computer Science from Concordia University of Montreal in 2003. Before joining UVic, he was a software engineer for Ericsson Inc, and Assistant Professor at Suffolk University in Boston. His main research is on theoretical and practical aspects of semistructured and graph databases, with a current focus on social and biological networks, automata-based techniques, and index structures for textual data.